Excel

YEAR 9

English Workbook

ESSENTIAL skills

Get the Results You Want!

PASCAL PRESS

Kristine Brown

Reprinted 2001, 2002, 2003, 2004, 2005, 2006, 2008, 2009, 2010

Updated in 2012 for the Australian Curriculum

Reprinted 2014, 2015, 2016, 2017, 2019, 2021 (twice), 2022

Updated in 2024 for the NSW Curriculum and Australian Curriculum Version 9.0 changes

ISBN 978 1 74020 038 7

Pascal Press
PO Box 250
Glebe NSW 2037
(02) 9198 1748
www.pascalpress.com.au

Publisher: Vivienne Joannou
Project editor: Mark Dixon
Edited by Valerie Marlborough and Frances Wade
Typeset by The Type Group and Grizzly Graphics (Leanne Richters)
Cover by DiZign Pty Ltd
Printed by Vivar Printing/Green Giant Press

CONTENTS

Guide to writing skills, punctuation and grammar

Chapter	Writing skills	Punctuation	Grammar
1 **Basic essay**	Basic essay structure Topic sentences	Commas (to break up lists)	The basic sentence (verbs, nouns, pronouns)
2 **Discussion essay**	Essay map Modality (in 'Writing paragraphs and whole texts')	Commas (to break up sentences)	Adjectives and adverbs
3 **Personal recount**	Structure and content of a recount Connectives (in 'Writing paragraphs and whole texts')	Commas (to separate linking words)	Sentences and subjects
4 **Instructions**	Using layout and highlighting	Commas (general revision)	Clauses (simple and compound sentences)
5 **Book report**	Paragraph organisation Present tense to retell events	Quotation marks (titles)	Clause and complex sentences
6 **Description of a scene**	Use of pronouns	Apostrophes (apostrophes of omission: *its* and *it's*)	Phrases
7 **Short story**	Story orientations	Apostrophe of possession	Non-finite ~*ing* clauses
8 **News article**	Structure of a news report—order of information	Quotation marks (exact words)	Verbs—past tense forms
9 **Blogpost/Letter to the editor**	Persuasive language devices Tone	Capital letters (proper names and titles)	Dependent clauses
10 **Biography**	Biography content Time connectives	Commas (revision)	Cohesion—using pronouns to link ideas
11 **Speech**	Opening paragraphs Rhetorical questions	Punctuating speeches	Spoken and written language
12 **Advertisement**	Drafting and revising to shorten	Punctuating advertisements	Leaving out words (in advertisements)
13 **Explanation**	Cohesive devices	Brackets (to include extra pieces of information)	Active and passive voice of the verb
14 **Factual report**	Generic noun forms	References (to books and websites)	Conjunctions and connectives
15 **Poem**	Alliteration Cohesion of ideas	Punctuating poems	Similes and metaphors

To the student

This book aims to give you practical help with the writing tasks you will do in Year 9 and later years at school. It is organised into fifteen chapters with each chapter focusing on a different text type (e.g. essays, book reviews and speeches). The topics and text types are meant to cover writing you might do across **all school subjects**—not just English.

The book is based on the understanding that we write differently depending on:

- our **purpose** in writing
- our **audience** and
- the **subject** we are writing about.

These three important considerations determine the way we organise the ideas in our writing, and the language we choose to express them.

Because of this, a key feature of the book is the use of models of different text types. You will find the model text on the first page of each chapter. On each side of the text, you will see notes about its overall structure and the language used. You should always read the model text and the notes very carefully. They are the basis of the activities in the chapter. When you are set a similar writing task at school, you should use the model pages to help you organise and express your ideas.

Another important feature of the book is the answer section. This section is more detailed than in many other books. This is for two reasons. Firstly, you may be working on your own when using the book. Secondly, the exercises are designed to teach you about writing rather than test what you already know. You should, of course, try to do the exercises on your own first, but if you are stuck, the answer section will help you.

The book provides a variety of exercise types. Some focus on words and sentences, but others give you guidance with larger chunks of text—paragraphs and whole texts. These provide you with additional models of the text type. Make sure you do **all** these exercises. You will improve your writing only by getting lots of practice.

Each chapter includes a vocabulary list. The words in the list are always taken from the chapter model text. Always look back to see the way the words are used in the text, before learning to spell them. Make it a goal to memorise all the spellings by the time you have finished the chapter.

Many exercises involve the use of a good dictionary or thesaurus. You could also use an online dictionary or thesaurus for word meanings—or just google them. These exercises are designed so that, even if you do not get all the correct answers, you will learn a lot along the way—about language, and about how to effectively use these important resources when writing.

The information in the sections headed 'Focus on punctuation' and 'Grammar' is very important. It will help you to write easy-to-understand and grammatically correct sentences. Be sure to read **all** this information.

Finally, the book is a resource to use whenever you write. Open it up and use it whenever you are doing your school assignments.

I very much hope you enjoy using the book.

Kristine Brown

CHAPTER 1

Basic essay

Outline three ways in which sport brings us benefits. (300 words)

Not everybody likes sport but most people agree that participation in sporting activity benefits us in many ways. The most obvious advantages are physical, but there are also social and personal benefits.

In the first place, all sport involves regular physical activity and, because of this, it helps us become healthier and fitter. Regular activity, for example, develops muscle tone and therefore improves body strength. It also fosters good breathing techniques and so improves our lung capacity. Furthermore, it reduces the risk of heart disease and high blood pressure. Also, because exercise burns up fat, sport is an ideal way to maintain a good body weight. This, in turn, is important for the prevention of other health problems.

Secondly, sport brings us many social benefits. Many people, for example, form strong and lasting friendships through participation in sport. It also teaches important lessons for getting on with others. These include sportsmanship, leadership and the importance of teamwork.

Thirdly, sport helps us develop personally—that is, mentally and emotionally. One of its most valuable aspects is that it teaches us to deal with both winning and losing. Some people believe competition is a bad thing, but if it teaches this important lesson it can be extremely useful. Another personal benefit is that it provides an opportunity to set and achieve goals. For some people this might mean winning medals and breaking records, but for most, it means striving for their 'personal best'.

These are just some of the advantages of participating in sport. Most sportsmen and sportswomen probably do not consciously think of these benefits when they play sport. Like me, they play sport for one simple reason—it is good fun.

STRUCTURE

overall structure reflects text purpose—to present information in an easy-to-follow format

All essays have this basic structure:

introduction, which includes:
- *a lead-in idea (not essential)*
- *a statement of essay question*
- *indication to the reader of what you are going to talk about—an 'essay map'*

one paragraph per main idea

topic sentences which tell the reader what the paragraph is about

development of main idea with examples, argument etc.

conclusion:
- *sums up content*
- *gives no new information*
- *gives writer's view of the topic in some way*

LANGUAGE FEATURES

the writer keeps a distance from the topic—not personal feelings and experiences

formal, not informal, everyday language

linking words, e.g. 'also', 'secondly'

many nouns such as 'sportsmanship', 'importance' etc. help us pack a lot of meaning into a sentence

often the use of 'we' or 'us' to talk about people in general

talking about people in general, not individuals

complete sentences

Comprehension

This section will check that you have understood the content of the text, but it will also help you to focus on the way the writer has organised and expressed his or her ideas.

1 What does the essay question ask the student to write about? Underline the correct answer.

a the benefits of sport

b the advantages and disadvantages of sport

c different types of sport we can play

2 What three broad benefits of sport does the essay focus on?

____

3 According to the writer, what three social lessons can sport teach us?

____

4 This sentence is missing from the text. Where does it belong? Underline the correct answer.

A small improvement in speed or distance or strength is enough to give them a great thrill.

a end of paragraph 2 **b** end of paragraph 3 **c** end of paragraph 4

5 In paragraph 4, what does *this important lesson* mean? Underline the correct answer.

a dealing with winning and losing **b** the value of competition **c** setting and achieving goals

6 Does the writer play sport? Which words tell you this most clearly.

____

Writing skills

Many essay questions ask you to argue a point of view, but some do not. Instead they ask you to explain or elaborate on a fact or accepted opinion (like this one here on sport). The **basic structure**, however, remains the same in all essays: introduction paragraph, body paragraphs, conclusion paragraph.

1 Underline the words in the introduction that tell the reader the topics of the three body paragraphs.

Topic sentences are the sentences in a paragraph that tell you what the paragraph is about. Often a topic sentence is the first sentence. In an essay, topic sentences are very important in helping your reader see how your ideas are connected to the main essay topic. They very often link up with ideas mentioned in the introduction.

2 Underline the topic sentence in each body paragraph.

a Do the topic sentences match the order in which the topics are mentioned in the introduction? Yes/No

b Do you think this is a good idea and if so, why?

____

____

3 There are many words in this essay that link the ideas in one sentence to the ideas in another, e.g. *also, however, firstly*. Underline all examples of these types of words.

4 The three sentences below were in the first draft of this essay, but the writer rewrote them in the final draft. Underline the rewritten sentences, and then say why the writer decided to rewrite them.

a *I know a lot of people who don't like sport but most of them think it is good for you.*

b *It helps you breathe better.*

c *I have made a lot of friends through sport.*

____

____

____

____

5 It is easy to take notes from a well-written essay because it has a clear structure. On your own paper, take notes now from this essay. Only write down the main ideas and the examples given. Here is the beginning of one student's notes to help you:

Sport benefits us:

- *physically because involves regular physical activity*
  - *develops muscle tone—improves body strength*
  - *fosters good breathing—improves lung capacity*
  - *reduces ...*

Vocabulary

participation	**benefits**	**obvious**	**advantages**	**physical**
involve	**healthier**	**muscle**	**fosters**	**techniques**
capacity	**disease**	**maintain**	**prevention**	**valuable**
aspects	**competition**	**extremely**	**striving**	**consciously**

A good method of learning the spellings of words is the Look, Cover, Write, Check method.

Look: Study the word closely, paying special attention to the difficult parts (e.g. silent letters).
Cover: Cover the word and try to see it with your mind's eye.
Write: Write the word without looking back.
Check: Check your spelling. If it is not correct, repeat the process.

This method is better than simply copying the words because your mind is actively trying to remember. Use this method now to learn the words in the list.

Look again now at the words above and choose the five that give you the most trouble. Write these words out again in the space below. Look back at them from time to time as you do the activities on this page, to help commit them to your memory.

____

Focus on punctuation

Commas

Commas help to make your meaning clear to your reader and so are very important. Commas are used for many purposes. One purpose is to break up the items in a 'list' of three or more items, e.g. *These include sportsmanship, leadership and the importance of teamwork.*

Usually a comma is not needed before *and* or *or* at the end of a list of items, but sometimes one is needed, especially if some items in the list consist of more than one word.

1 Use commas to break up the lists in these sentences.

a Lack of exercise increases the risk of heart disease muscular injury and back pain.

b Walking jogging swimming skipping cycling and dancing all make the body work at a steady rhythmic pace.

c If you have back pain you should be careful when lifting or carrying objects exercising or sitting.

d Team sports such as hockey netball soccer basketball and cricket encourage the development of important social skills.

2 Which of the sentences below is punctuated correctly?

a The coach stressed the importance of fitness practice, and commitment.

b The coach stressed the importance of fitness, practice and commitment.

c The coach stressed the importance of fitness practice and commitment.

d The coach stressed the importance of fitness, practice, and commitment.

Select a word

Choose words from the vocabulary list that mean the same as these words.

1 keep ______________________

2 trying ______________________

3 areas or parts ______________________

4 clearly able to be seen ______________________

5 encourages, helps the development of ______________________

6 knowingly ______________________

7 ability to contain an amount ______________________

8 stopping or avoiding ______________________

Grammar

The basic sentence

- A sentence is a group of words that express a complete thought.
- A sentence must have a verb. Some sentences consist of a verb only, e.g.
  Start! Help!
- Verbs very often consist of more than one word—this is a verb group, e.g.
  is starting, have helped, will start, have been helping, does help, can't start
- Most sentences also have a noun that is the subject of the verb—that is, what the sentence is about, e.g.
  The coach helps. The game is starting.
- Sometimes the subject will be a pronoun, which takes the noun's place (e.g. *she* instead of *Mum*), e.g.
  He helps. It is starting.
- Sentences in essays are usually longer and more complicated than this, but in all cases they must have a subject and a verb and express a complete thought.
- Important: *~ing* words are only part of the verb. If a group of words has only an *~ing* form of the verb it is not a complete sentence, e.g.
  Playing sport. This is not a sentence
  He was playing sport. This is a sentence.

1 In these sentences

i underline the verb group

ii circle the noun or pronoun that is the subject of the sentence,
e.g. (Sport) develops our bodies.

a Stress can be dangerous.

b Heart disease is the most common cause of death.

c Children get a lot of exercise naturally.

d Regular exercise relieves stress.

2 Are the following groups of words sentences or not? If they are not, change them to make them a sentence.

e.g. *Children liking sport.* (This is not a sentence because this is only the *~ing* form of the verb. One way to change it is *Children like sport.*)

- **a** Breathing deeply.
- **b** Check your pulse.
- **c** Aerobic means 'with air'.
- **d** Being a very fit person.
- **e** She plays sports regularly.

____

____

3 Sentences don't have to be long to be complete sentences, and all long strings of words are not necessarily complete sentences. Write S for Sentence and NS for Not a Sentence after each example below.

- **a** Having the chance to play sports regularly and often at school. ______
- **b** Year 9 students win. ______
- **c** Confidence helps. ______
- **d** Being confident helps. ______
- **e** Encouraging everyone to attend or take part in every match at our school. ______
- **f** Winning some and losing some but mostly just enjoying the competition. ______
- **g** Having a good attitude. ______
- **h** Enjoying sport is probably the most important element. ______

Word study

Longer nouns made from verbs help you to pack more meaning into a sentence.
Make nouns from these verbs.

1	participate	*participation*	**2**	involve	*involvement*
3	reduce	______	**4**	improve	______
5	develop	______	**6**	value	______
7	relax	______	**8**	protect	______
9	treat	______	**10**	exercise	______

Evaluating other people's writing

What is wrong with the student's essay below? Mark at least five things in the essay that could be improved, e.g.

- essay structure
- vocabulary and grammar
- punctuation

(Use the model essay and the structure and language feature notes to help you.)

> I like sport. It does you a lot of good especially physically. Physically it develops your muscles, bones, breathing. Also it takes off weight if you are overweight. It can be good for your social life too.

It helps you to meet people and to have a good time. Some of my best friends are from sports I have played. I have played tennis soccer and athletics during high school. These were all good fun and good for me too. I know that I am stronger and fitter than many others.

Even if you do not like sport I think you should try it. Because once you start you get involved and it does not matter if you are no good. The important thing is playing fair and working with your team-mates.

Sport brings us many benefits.

Quick think

How much do you know about sport and exercise? Are the following true or false?

1 Disease of the heart and blood vessels accounts for one-half of male deaths between the ages of 30 and 64 years. ______________________

2 The normal resting pulse rate is 60–80 beats a minute. ______________________

3 More fat is burned through vigorous short exercise (e.g. squash) than during long endurance activities (e.g. swimming, walking). ______________________

4 Crash diets cause a reduction in muscle tissue as well as fat. ______________________

Proofreading

Find the four incomplete sentences in this paragraph. Make them complete by adding a subject, adding a verb, or changing the verb.

In many sports the notion of 'personal best' is very important. Meaning beating your previous best effort. In athletics, runners, for example, try to beat their best times over a distance and long jumpers try to beat their best distance jumped. The same in swimming. Swimmers are always talking about their PB. Being a short way of saying 'personal best'. This focus on beating yourself rather than others is a very healthy one. Stopping many athletes from becoming downhearted about not always winning.

____

____

____

Writing paragraphs and whole texts

1 Put the sentences in the right order to make a paragraph that could be used in an essay on this topic. Use the words in italics to help you.

a *However*, it is not necessary to win to enjoy sport.

b *Winning a race or beating another team* is certainly exciting and for most people leads to a sense of achievement.

c Of course, you are unlikely to get *this feeling* if you do not give your best.

d *Even when you come second or even last*, you will probably feel a sense of achievement just by competing and giving your best.

e One of the best parts of playing sport is the enjoyment that comes from *playing well*.

____

It is important to make your paragraphs cohesive—that is, to make them 'hang together' around one idea. Think about how you did this activity. You could only do it because the writer has used language that helped you follow the ideas from one sentence to the next, and to see the main idea in them all.

2 Look at this student's notes for an essay on the same topic as the model essay. Write a paragraph using these notes. Follow the pattern of the paragraphs in the model essay.

- *teaches the importance of teamwork*
  - *team games, e.g. football, netball*
  - *relays in swimming and athletics*
- *we learn*
  - *to trust team-mates*
  - *that individuals are all different—different strengths and weaknesses*
  - *to always do our best because others depend on you—this teaches responsibility*
- *teamwork possibly one of the most important things sport develops*

3 Make notes like those above for a paragraph on *one* benefit of sport. It may be an idea mentioned in this chapter or something else. Begin with the main idea (or benefit) and then expand on it with evidence and examples that explain the idea further.

Now expand your notes into a paragraph.

4 In a basic essay like the one at the beginning of this chapter, you have to accept the point of view in the essay question (in this case, that sport brings us benefits) and illustrate it with examples. However, in the conclusion you should restate and expand at least a little on this view using your own ideas and words.

a Read the conclusion of the model essay again.

b Think about your own overall view on the benefits of sport.

c In the space below, draft a short conclusion for an essay on the topic that reflects your view.

5 For extra writing practice, write your own 300-word essay on the chapter topic. You can use the paragraphs from Activities 2 and 3 and the short conclusion you drafted in Activity 4. You only have to add an introduction and perhaps one other body paragraph. Use the space below for any notes or drafting.

CHAPTER 2

Discussion essay

'Girls and boys should be educated separately in secondary school.' Discuss. (350 words)

STRUCTURE

overall structure reflects text purpose—to discuss an issue and put forward a point of view

introduction, which includes:
- *lead-in idea (optional)*
- *essay question*
- *'essay map' (generally no view at this stage—view comes at end)*

balanced discussion of issue

paragraphs, which give arguments for or against

(some discussion essays are not clearly 'for' and 'against'—they are a general discussion of ideas)

topic sentences

conclusion:
- *sums up content*
- *gives no new information*
- *states view on essay question (for, against or some position in between)*

When children reach the end of primary school, one important question their parents have to consider is whether it would be better to send them to a single-sex school or a mixed-sex (coeducational) school. They have to weigh up many points on both sides of the argument—both educational and social.

One of the main arguments for segregated education is the view that boys demand more of their teachers' time. Firstly, boys can require more discipline because they are more likely to misbehave in class. Secondly, they tend to get more attention than girls because they speak up more in class. If girls are educated separately, they might have more of their teachers' time, and so learn faster and better.

Another argument for separate schooling is that it gives students a better chance to do well in subjects which traditionally have been thought to be either feminine or masculine interests. For example, girls sometimes might not even try to do well in maths and science because they think boys are better at these subjects. Similarly boys might not try to do well in expressive subjects such as English because they think girls are more interested in these subjects. If they are in segregated classes, they may not be so affected by these ideas and might be more likely to perform at their best.

These arguments may appear strong reasons to send a girl or boy to a single-sex school, but there are also reasons to favour mixed-sex schooling. The strongest argument is that it prepares students better for the real world, especially the world of work where in general people have to work with both sexes. Both males and females need to learn to get on with one another, and school is probably the best place to learn these important social skills.

Another argument in favour of coeducation is that both boys and girls can have a positive effect on the classroom. For example, boys may behave more appropriately if there are girls in the classroom and girls may learn to be more outspoken if they see boys behaving in this way.

Overall the social arguments for combined schooling outweigh the mostly educational arguments for segregated schooling. Education is not only about learning facts and figures but also about learning how to survive socially. Coeducation is certainly the best system for teaching this important lesson.

LANGUAGE FEATURES

distance from the topic—not personal

formal language

no emotional language

linking words, (also called connectives), e.g. 'firstly', 'secondly'

talking about people in general, not individual, e.g. 'girls', 'boys', 'teachers'

words such as 'may', can' and 'probably' reflect that the issue is debatable—not black and white

pronouns to link ideas, e.g. 'they', 'these'

complete sentences

Comprehension

Remember, working your way through the text to answer these questions will help you understand the organisation of ideas in the essay.

1 What does the essay question ask the student to do? Underline the correct answer.

- **a** Explain the advantages of single-sex education.
- **b** Put forward a point of view on the advantages of single-sex education.
- **c** Discuss points of view both for and against the idea of single-sex education.

2 What two positive aspects of single-sex education does the writer mention?

____

____

3 What two positive aspects of coeducation does the writer mention?

____

____

4 According to the writer, why are girls likely to do better in maths and science in single-sex schools?

____

5 According to the writer, how does mixed-sex schooling prepare students for the world of work?

____

6 Underline the correct answer. Does the writer:

- **a** agree with the statement 'Girls and boys should be educated separately in secondary school'?
- **b** disagree with the statement 'Girls and boys should be educated separately in secondary school'?
- **c** have a view somewhere in between?

Writing skills

1 When writing essays, it is good to state the essay topic in slightly different words from the question. Underline the words used in the introduction that do this.

2 Good essay introductions usually give the reader an idea of the points that will follow in the body paragraphs. The second sentence of this essay introduction does this (see the 'essay map').

Sometimes the essay map says exactly what the following points will be and sometimes it only gives a general idea. Is the essay map in this essay exact or general? ______________

Which two words in the essay map of this essay tell you the kinds of ideas that will be discussed?

____

Discussion essays must be balanced, putting forward ideas on both sides of an issue. Even if you clearly feel more strongly on one side of the issue or the other, you must show that you have considered both sides of the argument.

3 Underline the sentence that tells you the writer is moving from the arguments *for* segregated schools to the arguments *against* them.

____

4 This paragraph is missing from the text. Where does it belong? Underline the correct answer.

Another argument for single-sex schools is both boys and girls learn more because they are not distracted by the other sex. They do not spend time thinking about how they look or whether or not someone they like is in their class. In my experience this is definitely a distraction to learning for many students.

a after paragraph 1 (the introduction) **b** after paragraph 4 **c** after paragraph 3

5 Underline the topic sentence in each body paragraph.

6 The three sentences below were in the first draft of this essay, but the writer rewrote them in the final draft. Underline the rewritten sentences, and then say why the writer decided to rewrite them.

a *I don't think it is cool being good at maths and science in front of boys.*

b *I reckon it is better to go to mixed school.*

c *So many boys I know at single-sex schools have absolutely no idea how to behave with girls.*

____

____

____

7 Remember: It is easy to take notes from a good essay because it is so clearly organised. On your own paper, take brief notes from this essay. Write down only:

- the question under discussion
- the points for
- the points against
- the writer's conclusion

Vocabulary

consider	**coeducational**	**weigh up**	**argument**	**social**
segregated	**discipline**	**misbehave**	**appropriately**	**separately**
traditionally	**feminine**	**masculine**	**expressive**	**affected**
favour	**effect**	**outweigh**	**figures**	**system**

Write out the words in the above list and underline the parts that you think are most difficult to spell, e.g. the 'c' in *discipline* may be difficult to remember because it is not heard clearly as a 'c'.

Now write them out again using the Look, Cover, Write, Check method.

Take special note of the words in the list that end in *~ly*: *traditionally*, *appropriately* and *separately*. These are all adverbs made from adjectives. If the base adjective ends in 'al', you must double the 'l' before adding the *~ly*. If the adjective ends in 'e', you must keep the 'e' before adding the *~ly*.

Focus on punctuation

Commas

Commas are used to break up long sentences into two or three 'chunks'. This helps us understand their meaning, e.g.

If girls are educated separately, they will have more of their teachers' time, and so learn faster and better.

Reading the sentences out loud with expression can help you sense where a comma is needed.

1 Use commas to break up these sentences into 'chunks' of meaning to make them clearer.

a Some schools have introduced single-sex classes and these seem to be successful with girls.

b One study investigated the experiences of both boys and girls in schools and found that many unexpected aspects of school were affected by gender.

c Some school systems in Australia have gender policies in place but there are differences in the way these policies are implemented.

d One study showed that boys claimed two-thirds of a teacher's attention mainly because they needed more discipline.

2 Which sentence below shows the best use of commas to make the meaning clear?

a Students in some schools are broken into same-sex classes for maths and English and although it is a timetabling challenge, there appear to be some benefits in learning for both sexes.

b Students in some schools are broken into same-sex classes for maths and English, and although it is a timetabling challenge there appear to be some benefits in learning for both sexes.

c Students in some schools, are broken into same-sex classes for maths and English, and although it is a timetabling challenge, there appear to be some benefits in learning for both sexes.

d Students in some schools are broken into same-sex classes for maths and English, and although it is a timetabling challenge, there appear to be some benefits in learning for both sexes.

Select a word

Choose words from the vocabulary list that mean the same as these words.

1 separated ____________________

2 suitably ____________________

3 support, be on the side of ____________________

4 think about ____________________

5 are stronger than ____________________

6 in the past ____________________

7 method ____________________

8 in a manner suited to the situation ____________________

Grammar

Adjectives and adverbs

Remember:

- A sentence is a group of words that express a complete thought. All sentences must have a verb (e.g. *Start*) and most sentences also have a noun or pronoun as subject (e.g. *You start*).
- *~ing* words are only part of the verb, so *Going to school* is <u>not</u> a sentence, but *He is going to school* or *He goes to school* is a sentence.
- Most sentences also contain other types of words (or parts of speech), e.g.
  - **adjectives**—words that describe a noun, e.g. *good, local, popular.*

    He goes to a <u>good</u> school.
    He goes to the <u>local</u> school.

    <u>Single-sex</u> classes are <u>popular</u>.
  - **adverbs**—words that tell you something extra about the verb or adjective, e.g. *usually, socially.*

    Many adverbs end in *~ly*.
    Students <u>usually</u> go to local schools.
    Students may benefit <u>socially</u> in mixed schools.
- Some adjectives identify or quantify a noun, e.g. the *fourth* photo, the *middle* one, *several* people.

1 In these sentences underline any adjectives and draw a line to the noun each one describes, e.g.

<u>Single-sex</u> classes are <u>popular</u>.

a I think there are social benefits.

b Students can be distracted by the opposite sex.

c Academic achievement is an important issue.

d My local school is coeducational.

2 In these sentences underline any adverbs and draw a line to the verb or adjective each one tells you something extra about, e.g. *Parents have to choose carefully.*

a Do you think students benefit educationally? b Schools often offer single-sex classes.

c My sister happily attended a single-sex school for six years.

d Students sometimes have to travel long distances to find a single-sex school.

3 In which sentence are the adjectives and adverbs used correctly?

a Changes to school systems must be made slow and carefully and only after extensive research.

b Changes to school systems must be made slow and careful and only after extensive research.

c Changes to school systems must be made slowly and carefully and only after extensively research.

d Changes to school systems must be made slowly and carefully and only after extensive research.

Word study

Which one to use—*affect* or *effect*?

- *Affect* is a verb, e.g. *The noise in the classroom affects their ability to concentrate.*
- *Effect* is a usually a noun, e.g. *The effect on the girls was terrible.*

Choose the right word and add endings (*~s, ~ing, ~ed*) where needed.

1 Different schools ____________________ students in different ways.

2 The teacher liked the ____________________ it had on the boys.

3 What ____________________ did the school have on you?

4 She was terribly ____________________ by the bad news.

5 The travel is ____________________ my health.

6 The positive ____________________ of single-sex schooling are still not clear.

Evaluating other people's writing

What is wrong with the student's discussion essay below? Mark at least five things in the essay that could be improved, e.g.

- essay structure
- vocabulary and grammar
- punctuation

I go to an all-girls school and I find it very good. There are many advantages I can see. In the first place, you don't have to worry so much about how you look. I have friends at the coeducational school in the next suburb who spend all their time thinking about how to look good while still wearing the school uniform. I could not stand this. I am not sure if boys do this too, but I think it a very strong reason to go to single-sex schools.

Another reason is that you do not have to waste all that time waiting for the boys to settle down in class. Do you remember primary school? I do. It used to take 5 minutes at least to get everyone quiet before you could do any work. That does not happen in our school. Girls are just so much better behaved I reckon. That is why I think my parents wanted me to go to this school.

I actually can't think of any advantages of mixed-sex schools but I suppose there are some. Well, you meet more boys of course. But I don't think that is what this essay is supposed to be about.

In conclusion, as you can clearly see, I think the question is right. We should be educated separately.

Quick think

Like many languages, the English language 'borrows' words from other languages. The essay refers to 'feminine and 'masculine' interests. There is a borrowed word for an extremely masculine way of behaviour that you may have heard: *macho. Macho* is borrowed from Mexican Spanish and means a man who displays *machismo* or strong masculinity.

Can you match these groups of words with the countries they come from? Thinking about the look and meanings of the group of words should help you.

Word groups		Country of origin	
1	desperado, siesta, mosquito	a	Italian
2	yoga, bungalow, shampoo, verandah	b	Dutch
3	gourmet, amateur, premiere, camouflage	c	Spanish
4	skipper, deck, yacht	d	Indian (Hindi)
5	studio, volcano, casino, inferno, broccoli	e	Arabic
6	sofa, assassin, algebra	f	French

Proofreading

Correct the spelling mistakes. Check your corrections against the chapter vocabulary list.

coeducational	argumant	social	segragated
disipline	misbihave	appropriatly	seperately
traditionaly	feminine	masculin	espressive
favor	efect	outweigh	sistem

Writing paragraphs and whole texts

The term **modality** refers to the way we show by our language how certain or strongly we feel about ideas.

One way we do this is with modal verbs—small verbs such as *may, might, can, could, should, must, ought to, will* and *would*.

Another way is with adjectives such as *possible, definite, sure* and *probable* and their adverbial forms *possibly, definitely, surely* and *probably*.

The discussion essay on page 10 uses modal forms to reflect that the issue is debatable and to show the writer knows the points do not necessarily refer to every group of students or schools. For example, 'boys can require more discipline' (that is, some boys might but not all do).

1 In essays you often need to write about ideas that are not absolutely certain or 'black and white'. It is important to show the reader how certain or committed you are to each idea.

For each pair of sentences below, tick the one that shows the most certainty or strength of feeling.

a i Segregation may benefit girls in subjects where boys traditionally do well. ______
ii Segregation will benefit girls in subjects where boys traditionally do well. ______

b i Research should be done before any changes to the system. ______
ii Research could be done before any changes to the system. ______

c i My experience showed me the possible advantages of single-sex schools. ______
ii My experience showed me the clear advantages of single-sex schools. ______

2 Put these sentences in order from the one that shows you are most certain and committed (1) to the one that shows you are least certain (6). (There may be more than one right answer.)

a Girls' self-esteem increases in single-sex schools.

b Girls' self-esteem probably increases in single-sex schools.

c Girls' self-esteem possibly increases in single-sex schools.

d Girls' self-esteem may increase in single-sex schools.

e Girls' self-esteem certainly increases in single-sex schools.

f It is said that girls' self-esteem increases in single-sex schools.

____

3 Put these sentences in the right order to make a paragraph that could be used in an essay on the model essay topic. Use the words in *italics* to help you.

a *In general*, the girls seem to like the classes very much, because they find it easier to work without boys.

b One way to get the best of both single-sex and mixed-sex schooling might be for schools to offer *single-sex classes*.

c One survey found that *boys* could see no educational point in single-sex classes at all.

d Many schools in fact have tried *this* (mainly maths and science classes for girls) and have reported quite positive *results*.

e *Furthermore*, they did not like the idea of being separated from girls.

f *However*, while the girls like them, the boys often do not.

____

4 Write a plan for a discussion essay on the topic 'We should not have to wear school uniforms' using the essay in this unit as a model.

____

____

____

____

____

____

____

____

____

When you have completed your plan, write:

- a short introduction
- a topic sentence for each body paragraph
- a short conclusion stating your overall opinion.

5 For extra writing practice, write the whole essay for the school uniforms topic. You are almost there already if you have done exercise 4 above. You only have to complete the body paragraphs and you are done. Use the space below for any further notes or drafting.

CHAPTER 3

Personal recount

STRUCTURE

overall structure reflects text

purpose—to retell past events or experiences

orientation to events, e.g. when and where they happened, who was involved

retelling of series of events usually in order that they occurred in real world

may be a comment on events at various points, especially at the end

some details to add interest or humour

LANGUAGE FEATURES

past tense, e.g. 'was', 'loaded'

many action verbs, e.g. 'arrived', 'poured'

linking words and phrases which show time sequence, e.g. during the day, by the second last visit

specific reference to people and things, e.g. 'Donna Squires'

first person personal pronouns, e.g. 'we', 'ourselves'

Adventure World—Design and Technology excursion

It was a cold but refreshing morning on 21 August as Year 9 were loaded onto the buses that would take us to our destiny, Adventure World. En route, we were blessed with the voices of a host of angels … and one Daniel Everson. When we arrived, we poured out of the buses and waited for what seemed like forever to receive our tickets and instructions about our assignment. We were to work hard and were not allowed to enjoy ourselves! We had to slave away, recording the design of the park, testing the rides for faults, and generally not have a good time. During the day, there was an accident that involved Donna Squires, the Pirate Ship and an urgent need for a bucket. Otherwise, the day was a great experience for all of us and the teachers as well (even though, as already mentioned, *none* of us had a good time).

Josh Langerak

Down at the graveyard—Year 9 History excursion

One morning last term, we gathered up our courage, and prepared to walk to the graveyard of St Stephen's Church for our Year 9 history excursion. We were terrified by the belief that it was haunted by evil spirits. We were scared to tread anywhere near the graves, but we were more petrified by what we might face if we didn't finish our work.

So, after being handed a worksheet, we all selected our graves to study, took out our cameras and got to work. Each person had to study a grave, take photos of it from different angles and do some written work about the graveyard itself. To everyone's disappointment, the next day was too wet to go back but by the day after the weather had cleared. Putting our fears behind us, we set off and got to work again (well, most of us did). This continued for around two weeks straight, as we trekked to and from the graveyard each day. By the second last visit, most people had finished their work, with one person even finding time to do all her maths homework (there's no understanding some people).

As the last day of the assignment dawned, most people had overcome their fears that the graveyard was haunted. However, when our photos were developed, the few who still believed were given their proof! The same girl who did her maths homework had actually photographed a ghost! A chill went down our spines as we thought about how close we had come to meeting the dead. But just as everyone was enjoying a sense of relief that they had not been possessed, we were presented with the assignment sheets for the next historic outing!

Kieran Colreavy

Comprehension

1 Fill in the chart about each recount.

	Recount 1	Recount 2
When did the events take place?		
Where did they take place?		
Why did they take place?		
Who was involved?		

2 **Recount 1**

a What were the students doing on the bus trip?

b What do you think happened to Donna Squires?

c Why does the writer keep making comments about not having a good time?

3 **Recount 2**

a Why did the students have to gather up courage for the excursion?

b What was scarier than the graves?

c Do you think the writer really believes in ghosts? Give reasons for your opinion.

Writing skills

The **structure of a recount** is simple—basically a series of events in chronological order. However, you need to make your recount more than 'we did this, then we did that, then we did something else …'. To make a recount interesting, you must think carefully about the **content**—what to include and what not to include—and then find something interesting to say about what happened.

1 Both writers manage to tell us about many events in a short space and give us a good picture of what happened. How do they do this?

2 Underline the words or parts of the text that tell the reader when, and in which order, things happened.

3 Both writers use humour to make their recounts more interesting. Underline the humorous parts.

4 These sentences were in the first drafts of the recounts. Why do you think the writers left them out of the final drafts?

- **a** *Our group went first to the Demon ride.* (Recount 1)
- **b** *I am only joking—actually we had a very good time.* (Recount 1)
- **c** *History is my worst subject.* (Recount 2)
- **d** *I got my worst mark ever for this assignment.* (Recount 2)

____

____

____

____

Vocabulary

refreshing	**destiny**	**blessed**	**faults**	**generally**
urgent	**experience**	**courage**	**excursion**	**terrified**
haunted	**tread**	**petrified**	**angles**	**disappointment**
trekked	**developed**	**believers**	**chill**	**possessed**

One good technique for spelling words correctly is to write the word a few different ways on a scrap of paper to decide which way looks right, e.g.
~~*terified*~~*?* *terrified?* ~~*teriffied*~~*?*

Even if you don't always choose the correct one, this technique will develop your 'visual spelling sense', and you will get better at using it.

Learn the words using the Look, Cover, Write, Check method. Use the above technique with words you are unsure of.

Test your knowledge now on these difficult words. (Cover up the list while you do this.)

Which is the correct spelling? (Tick one.)

trekked	____	trecked	____	treked	____
experiense	____	experience	____	experence	____
currage	____	courage	____	curage	____
generally	____	genrally	____	generly	____
posessed	____	possessed	____	possesed	____
egsursion	____	excersion	____	excursion	____

Focus on punctuation

Commas

In the sentences below, a **comma** is used to separate a linking word or phrase from the rest of the sentence.

En route, we were blessed with the voices of a host of angels …
Otherwise, the day was a great experience for all of us …

Put commas into these sentences where needed to separate linking words or phrases.

1 Last month we went on an exciting three-day excursion to the Snowy Mountains.

2 Much to our surprise the day turned out better than expected.

3 Nevertheless the teachers said they had never been on such an enjoyable excursion.

4 After a long three hours we finally made it to the top of the cliff and saw the bus.

5 Finally we must say how great the new Year 7 kids were.

6 At the end of the four-day trek we emerged into the clearing and saw our anxious parents waiting at the pick-up point.

Select a word

Choose words from the vocabulary list that mean the same as these words.

1 needing sudden attention	____________	2 fate	____________
3 problems	____________	4 extremely frightened	____________
5 controlled by an evil spirit	____________	6 walked a long distance	____________
7 cold	____________	8 lucky	____________

Grammar

Sentences and subjects

- Remember: A **sentence** is a group of words that express a complete thought.
- All sentences have a **verb** and most sentences also have a **noun** or **pronoun** as the **subject** of the sentence. In command (**imperative**) sentences such as *Be careful* or *Watch this space*, the subject 'you' is understood by the listener/reader. Also in everyday speech we often omit the subject, e.g. *Want lunch now?* or *Done shopping*. Again the subject is understood.
- Often the subject of the sentence is more than one word. It is a noun with some other words attached—a **noun group**, e.g.
  The whole class enjoyed the experience. (Subject is the noun group *the whole class*)
  Driving back was a dreadful experience. (Subject is the noun group *driving back*)

1 In these sentences:
- underline the verb group
- circle the noun group that is the subject of these sentences,
  e.g. *(The end-of-year concert) took place on Friday, 13 December.*

a The Year 9 Food Technology class cooked for the parents.

b Peer Support leaders welcomed the new students.

c The annual walkathon got off to a great start at 9 a.m.

d The end point of the trip was the Warragamba Dam.

e A hearty lunch kept us going for the rest of the afternoon.

f Ten students from Year 9 took part in the concert.

g Having lunch at McDonald's and then some nap-time in the bus were the highlights of the trip for some people.

h Climbing the hill to the lookout was definitely not the best way to end the long day.

2 Write S for Sentence and NS for Not a Sentence after each example below.

a The funniest part of the trip at the end of a long day. ______

b The whole class feeling rather excited but scared at the same time. ______

c However, we all agreed the excursion was definitely worthwhile. ______

d Driving around endless curves in an oversize bus frightening us out of our wits. ______

e Sitting in the bus for five hours was not so much fun. ______

Word study

The writers use a number of everyday expressions to describe their experiences and feelings. Find these expressions in the text and look at how they are used:

poured out of the buses, to slave away (Recount 1)
gathered up our courage, got to work, putting our fears behind us, chill went down our spines (Recount 2)

What do the following expressions mean?

1 It made the hairs on the back of my neck stand on end. ______

2 I got goosebumps all over. ______

3 It made my flesh crawl. ______

4 We worked like Trojans. ______

5 We had to sink or swim. ______

6 We showed them what we were made of. ______

7 We were home and hosed. ______

8 The day got off to a good (or bad) start. ______

Evaluating other people's writing

What is wrong with the student's recount of a school excursion below? Mark five things that could be improved, e.g.

- content
- grammar and vocabulary
- organisation of information
- punctuation

We all met at the railway station at 9. Some people were late so we got off to a bad start. We were going to meet in the second carriage but it was full so we sat in a few different carriages, which was not much fun because we were not together.

We arrived at Olympic Park at about 10, and we walked to the pool. This part was pretty boring really. When we got to the pool, we changed and went into the water straight away. Some of us got into trouble for being a bit stupid but mostly things went pretty well and we had a good day. We were given a tour of the place after our swim and I liked that a lot. In fact it was the best part really. So, in conclusion, we had a pretty good day at the Olympic Park. I'd like to go again soon.

Quick think

Complete this crossword with words you might find in a recount of school activities or excursions.

Across

2 Although there were some problems, overall the day was a ____________.

4 pleased because something unpleasant has ended or not happened

8 It was a very positive ____________ for teachers and students.

10 a school task

12 She is usually girl champion at the swimming ____________.

13 every year

14 trip, travels

Down

1 We ____________ at 9 am and left at 12 noon.

3 shocked, amazed

5 It was difficult at first, but _________ we got there.

6 an order, how to do something

7 the way people behaved

9 at the end

11 at first

Proofreading

Correct the spellings where necessary. Write the word a few different ways to help you find the correct spelling. Check your corrections against the chapter vocabulary list.

refreshing	desteny	blessd	faults	genrally
urgent	expereince	curage	exursion	terified
haunted	tred	petrifyed	angles	disapointment
treked	developed	believers	chill	posessed

Writing paragraphs and whole texts

1 Can you sort this out? Below are two recounts (written by students Catherine Bendall and Hannah McLean) jumbled together. One is about a geography excursion, and the other is about a cross-country carnival. (The sentences are in the order in which they would occur in the two recounts.) Underline the sentences from the cross-country carnival recount.

On Monday, 21 September, our prayers were finally answered! The two Year 9 geography classes went on an excursion. Thursday, 30 April, was a day that stretched our calf muscles, our endurance and later our stomachs as, once again, PHS held its annual cross-country carnival. We spent the day visiting the Sydney Aquarium, watching movies at the Imax, chasing ducks in knee-deep water and generally wreaking havoc on the whole of Sydney! As usual, the day began early so that all races could be held before the now famous cross-country barbecue. One major disappointment was discovering the 3D movie was only 2D. The younger age groups ran first with some outstanding successes from newcomers to the school, Sophie Bromfield and Matt Stanowski. We can't, however, overlook the *educational* aspect of the excursion as numerous (ahem) students filled out their worksheets. Then it was the turn of the Under 15s with Tom Richardson (surprise, surprise) and Skye Blakeney breaking school records by several minutes. Congratulations to Ms Makis and Mr Maharaj, who managed to keep us under some sort of control and get us back alive and well! After a tough battle, Wentworth House finally won the day. The SRC barbecue proved to be a great success as usual, and was much appreciated by the runners, joggers (!) and spectators.

2 Sometimes at school you are asked to write imaginative recounts. For example, you may be asked to imagine a day in the life of someone who lived in a previous century.

This student (Rosie Brown) was asked to write a recount of a meeting with a Shakespearean character. Can you put the paragraphs in an order that makes sense? Here is the first paragraph to help you.

As I walked across the large wooden drawbridge, I reflected upon the fact that I was the first reporter ever to interview the great and courageous Thane Macbeth and his lovely lady. The footman intercepted me and said, 'Who goeth there?'

a I entered a large hall. Before me lay a scene of celebration and chaos. A beautifully decorated table stood in the middle. Servants were bustling around, perfecting the flower arrangements and polishing the armour until it sparkled.

b My shoes echoed loudly across the stone floors as the footman and I walked in silence through the halls and corridors of the castle. Suddenly I found myself opposite a large, green door. The footman grunted at me to stay, while he checked if I was permitted to enter. He returned and let me in.

c Suddenly I caught the eye of a handsome fellow wearing a skirt. He seemed, however, quite unselfconscious. He smiled and walked towards me. I realised he was the new Thane of Cawdor. I smiled and introduced myself. He answered simply, 'Macbeth'.

d I replied with dignity that I was the reporter for *Old Idea* and I was here to interview Thane and Lady Macbeth about Macbeth's new title 'Thane of Cawdor'. I was frisked for hidden weapons and then allowed entry.

e Macbeth was called to go, and so introduced me to his wife. She was the picture of royalty. Fanned, fed and waited upon by seven maids, she was the only calm person in the whole palace. A pack of dogs drooled at her feet, sometimes snapping their great jaws at the bits of food she dropped.

f In the two hours I spent with him he made me feel very welcome. We watched the entertainment rehearsing for the evening while I interviewed him. He said he was very thankful for his new position. 'Oh great happiness, I am a man most blessed.'

g Only minutes later she dismissed me with a wave of her hand. On my way out I was seen by the gracious Macbeth and bid farewell. I wished him good luck and was taken back to the drawbridge. As I walked across it I wondered how two people with such different personalities could love each other so much.

h I asked her how she felt about Macbeth being made the new Thane of Cawdor. She seemed unimpressed and said, 'My master hath but a golden heart which blunts his power'. I was slightly shocked by this remark and didn't feel comfortable proceeding with the topic.

3 Linking words (also called **connectives**) that show time and chronological order are important when writing recounts. Here are some examples:

beforehand, afterwards, firstly, secondly, finally, lastly, at the end, at first, to begin with, meanwhile, at last, simultaneously, suddenly, all of a sudden, at the same time, eventually, then, next, later, some time later

In the recount below, choose the best word or phrase from the three options given to write in the spaces.

Note: be sure to read through the whole recount first to get an idea of the overall content and time sequence.

Yesterday was the Year 9 art excursion to the Picasso exhibition. The day started badly. We were meant to be at the station to catch the train to the city at 8 o'clock but as usual a few people were late. We waited and waited for the last few people to arrive. ________________ (At the same time, Secondly, Meanwhile) five trains came and went. ________________ (Eventually, Lastly, At the end) everyone was there except for Jem Cola, who lives right nearby in Railway Parade.

Mrs Frank asked Carly and me to run to his house to get him. After knocking on his door for five minutes, we decided no-one was home and started to walk back to the station. ________________ (At last, Suddenly, Meanwhile) the door opened and Jem stood there, half-asleep and bleary-eyed and still in his pyjamas, looking a bit like a Picasso painting, Carly commented. ________________ (Simultaneously, All of a sudden, Eventually) we made him understand that he was meant to be at the station and pulled him out the door with his hair flying and his clothes half-on.

When we got back to the station, we discovered that a tree had fallen on the line and that no trains would be leaving for a whole hour. ________________ (At first, Suddenly, Next) Mrs Frank was very annoyed but ________________ (next, then, at last) she saw a teaching opportunity to while away the time. Aren't teachers just wonderful? We all had to do a Picasso-style sketch of something around us. Most of us drew Jem, who looked exactly like a Picasso picture by this time. Jem drew Carly with three heads. ________________ (Afterwards, At last, At the end) the train arrived and we were on our way.

The exhibition itself was awesome. ________________ (At the same time, In the end, Finally) we all agreed that we had a way to go before we were as good as Picasso. Mrs Frank said that this, at least, was a good result for the day.

4 Imagine you meet a character from a book or play you have read. Give a short recount of your meeting (about 200–300 words). Remember—the purpose of a recount is to tell what happened. Use your own paper.

5 Choose a school event or excursion you have recently experienced, and write a recount of it (about 200–300 words). Again, remember the purpose of a recount. Use your own paper.

CHAPTER 4

Instructions

STRUCTURE

overall structure reflects text purpose—to give information about what to do

goal or purpose of instructions

often headings and subheadings to indicate broad stages in more complex instructions

steps to achieve the goal

comments on the usefulness or significance of the instruction

detailed information about where, when and how things should be done

Keeping safe in the bush

Stage 1: Preparation

Planning to go into the bush this weekend? Preparation may save your life.

Firstly, recognise your limitations and remember that a bush kilometre is a different proposition from a map kilometre. Secondly, travel in a party of four. This allows one or two to go for help in an emergency. Thirdly, give details of your trip to your parents, police or rangers.

Finally, give serious thought to what to wear and take. Wear long trousers, a sweater, strong boots and a waterproof coat with a hood. Take a change of clothes, food, water and a sleeping bag (and tent if going overnight or into mountainous country). Also take a safety kit, which includes a map, compass, waterproof matches, solid fuel firelighter, a whistle, a mirror for emergency signalling, a notebook and pencil, a knife, a cup or container, water, sterilisation tablets, a first aid kit and a torch.

Stage 2: The trip

On your trip, the pace of the party should be regulated to suit every member. The whole party should rest periodically.

Always try to be aware of your rate of progress and direction of travel by frequent reference to your map and compass, or to the position of the sun when visible.

Mountain areas are prone to sudden changes in weather conditions, and danger of death from exposure is an ever-present hazard. If any signs of illness are apparent, the whole party should immediately pitch tents, and then put the victim into a sleeping bag before their body loses its ability to keep itself warm.

Stage 3: If you get lost

Don't panic! Sit down and try to plan logically the best route to safety. Mark the route you take by breaking green twigs, scratching arrows in the ground showing direction of travel, placing stones on logs, making footprints in mud, or attaching pieces of paper to tree branches. Leave a dated note at each camp indicating the direction you are taking next, and the names and physical conditions of party members. Do not walk at night or in sleet, snow or fog. Make as sheltered a camp as possible and light a fire before exhaustion sets in. Await the arrival of daylight or searchers.

LANGUAGE FEATURES

the reader is referred to directly, e.g. 'you', 'your' or not at all

linking words (connectives) to show time sequence, e.g. 'firstly', 'secondly' (often numbers to show sequence)

mainly action verbs to give instructions, e.g. 'take', 'wear'

some specialised technical terms

sometimes words such as 'should' and 'could' to give advice

'if ...', and 'when ...' phrases and clauses

present tense to show what people do

Comprehension

The essential purpose of instruction texts is to tell the reader about something he or she does not know about. Therefore, they should be easy to comprehend and clear in both structure and language. Answering the questions here should help you see how well these instructions were written.

1 Circle the pieces of information that were included in the instructions.

a what to wear on a trip to the bush

b how to recognise signs of exposure

c what to include in a safety kit

d what to do in case of an air search

e what to do in case of a bushfire

f what to do before you set off on a bush trip

2 What reasons are given for the following actions?

a travelling in a group of four ____________________

b taking a mirror ____________________

c putting an ill person into a sleeping bag and tent ____________________

3 Write these sentences from the text in your own words.

a *... remember that a bush kilometre is a different proposition from a map kilometre.*

b *... the pace of the party should be regulated to suit every member.*

c *... be aware of your rate of progress and direction of travel by frequent reference to your map and compass ...*

d *Mountain areas are prone to sudden changes in weather conditions ...*

____

____

____

____

4 This information is missing from the text. Mark an ✗ in the text where you would add it.

Signs that could lead to death from exposure are loss of muscular power, staggering, mental and physical lethargy, loss of judgement, change of personality, change of speech and vision defects.

5 Write down three new things you learned from these instructions.

____

____

Writing skills

1 The text at the beginning of the chapter shows three stages of 'Keeping safe in the bush', but the original text had a fourth stage also. Which of the following do you think was the fourth stage? Give reasons for your choice.

a Stage 4: The weather

b Stage 4: Air searches for lost persons

c Stage 4: Avoiding sunburn

d Stage 4: Tips for packing your backpack

____

____

____

2 Sentences in instructions very often start with a verb or have a verb very close to the start, e.g.

- *Secondly, travel in a party of four.*
- *Wear long trousers, a sweater ...*
- *Thirdly, give details of your trip to your parents, police or rangers.*

Find all the sentences that have this structure and underline the verbs. Why do you think this is a common sentence pattern in instructions?

____

____

____

____

3 Instructions can sometimes be made clearer by the use of **bold letters** or CAPITALISATION to highlight important words or main ideas. It is best, however, to keep such highlighting to short phrases, rather than whole sentences or long strings of words.

Look at Stage 3, which contains very important information, and choose four or five phrases to highlight. Write the phrases below.

____

____

4 These sentences were in the original draft of these instructions. Underline the sentences that replaced them in the final draft, and say why you think the writer decided to do this.

a *You probably know what you should take in a safety kit so I won't go into details here.*

b *Always try to be aware of where you are.*

c *It is not a good idea to panic.*

d *Not walking at night, in sleet, snow or fog.*

____

____

____

____

Vocabulary

recognise	**limitations**	**proposition**	**emergency**	**mountainous**
compass	**signalling**	**sterilisation**	**regulated**	**pace**
periodically	**reference**	**visible**	**prone**	**exposure**
hazard	**apparent**	**immediately**	**logically**	**sheltered**

Look at the *~ly* adverbs in the list. When we add *~ly* to an adjective to make it an adverb, we don't change the spelling of the adjective at all. We simply add the *~ly*.

- Adjectives ending in *~e* keep the *~e* and add *~ly*, e.g.
  immediate + ly = immediately
- However, adjectives ending in *~able* or *~ible* drop the 'e' before adding *~ly*, e.g.
  possible + ly = possibly; probable + ly = probably
- Adjectives ending in *~al*, keep the *~al* and add *~ly*. They end up with a double 'll', e.g.
  periodical + ly = periodically; logical + ly = logically

Make adverbs from these adjectives by adding *~ly*.

1 approximate	__________	2 definite	__________
3 essential	__________	4 personal	__________
5 principal	__________	6 considerable	__________
7 incredible	__________	8 natural	__________
9 entire	__________	10 simple	__________

Learn the other words in the list using the Look, Cover, Write, Check method.

Focus on punctuation

Commas

Remember: We use **commas** to divide up items in a list, to separate a linking word from the rest of the sentences, and to divide up a sentence into meaningful chunks.

1 Put commas into these two paragraphs from the instructions without looking back. Check your work against the original.

a Finally give serious thought to what to wear and take. Wear long trousers a sweater strong boots and a waterproof coat with a hood. Take a change of clothes food water and a sleeping bag (and tent if going overnight or into mountainous country). Also take a safety kit which includes a map compass waterproof matches solid fuel firelighter a whistle a mirror for emergency signalling a notebook and pencil a knife a cup or container water sterilisation tablets a first aid kit and a torch.

b Mountain areas are prone to sudden changes in weather conditions and danger of death from exposure is an ever-present hazard. If any signs of illness are apparent the whole party should immediately pitch tents and then put the victim into a sleeping bag before their body loses its ability to keep itself warm.

2 Tick the sentence that is correctly punctuated with commas.

a Finally, because your clothes are likely to become wet, dirty, torn or lost you should always take a spare set.

b Finally because your clothes are likely to become wet, dirty, torn or lost, you should always take a spare set.

c Finally, because your clothes are likely to become wet, dirty, torn or lost, you should always take a spare set.

d Finally, because your clothes are likely to become wet, dirty torn or lost, you should always take a spare set.

Select a word

Choose words from the vocabulary list that have the same meanings as these words.

1 danger	__________	2 every now and then	__________
3 controlled or adapted	__________	4 likely (to have or do)	__________
5 speed or rate	__________	6 matter	__________
7 able to be seen	__________	8 under cover	__________

Grammar

Clauses

Many sentences have only one unit of meaning—that is, one basic thought, e.g.
Preparation may save your life.
The whole party should rest periodically.

We call these **simple sentences**. They have only one **clause**—one unit of meaning.

- Many sentences have two or more clauses. Look at these:
  Mountain areas are prone to sudden changes in weather conditions, and danger of death from exposure is an ever-present hazard.
  Sit down and try to plan logically the best route to safety.
- We call these **compound sentences**. They have two equally important clauses. Each clause can stand alone and be understood.
- Where we have two clauses of equal importance we can join them with the **conjunctions** *and, but, or, nor, then, so and yet. (And, but* and *or* are the most important to remember.*)* If we do not use these conjunctions, we must use a full stop to break up the clauses.
- In formal writing we do not usually begin a sentence with *but*. Instead we use *however* to capture the same meaning, e.g.
  You can drink from some creeks, but many are no longer safe because of pollution.
  You can drink from some creeks. However, many are no longer safe because of pollution.

1 Underline the verbs in these sentences from 'Keeping safe in the bush'. Then decide if they are made up of one clause or two. Write 1 or 2.

- **a** Secondly, travel in a party of four. ________
- **b** Thirdly, give details of your trip to your parents, police or rangers. ________
- **c** Wear long trousers, a sweater, strong boots and a waterproof coat with a hood. ________
- **d** Don't panic! ________
- **e** Make as sheltered a camp as possible and light a fire before exhaustion sets in. ________

2 Correct these sentences by putting a full stop between the clauses, or by using *and, but* or *or* to link them.

- **a** It is important to have enough food when you go camping, you need to think carefully about how much you can carry.
- **b** Bring ingredients for a sandwich, make them up when you stop for a rest.
- **c** Marshmallows are fabulous to toast over a fire, hot chocolate is a great tea or coffee substitute.
- **d** Packets of soup are good for crisis times, they provide warmth and instant energy.
- **e** You should not take too much food with you, you don't have to starve and suffer.

3 Tick which of the sentences below are written correctly.

- **a** Muesli, cereal and fruit are ideal for breakfast. But breakfast bars can make a good substitute. ____
- **b** Muesli, cereal and fruit are ideal for breakfast, but breakfast bars can make a good substitute. ____
- **c** Muesli, cereal and fruit are ideal for breakfast, breakfast bars can make a good substitute. ____
- **d** Muesli, cereal and fruit are ideal for breakfast. However, breakfast bars can make a good substitute. ____

Word study

Some verbs and nouns often go together, e.g. *pitch tents*. We call these **collocations**.
Match the verbs (1–10) with the nouns (a–j) to make common collocations to do with camping. (There may be more than one possibility for some words.)

1	strike	**a**	firewood	**2**	make	**b**	the fire
3	fetch	**c**	a flare	**4**	boil	**d**	camp
5	keep up	**e**	attention	**6**	find	**f**	trouble
7	run into	**g**	energy	**8**	attract	**h**	shelter
9	send up	**i**	the billy	**10**	put out	**j**	camp

Evaluating other people's writing

What is wrong with the instructions below? Mark at least five things in the instructions that could be improved, e.g.

- organisation of ideas
- vocabulary and grammar
- punctuation

Keep warm. Get out of the wind. The wind can take 10 or 15 degrees off the temperature. This is called the wind chill factor. Find shelter or put up your tent. Another good idea is to put on more clothing. Not necessarily thicker clothes but layers. The more layers the better. Also long underwear. Did you know that a lot of heat escapes through your head? Well it does and so you should wear a hat. The other end of your body can get cold too, and if your feet are cold, you'll never feel warm. I usually wear two pairs of socks in cold weather. Staying close to a friend. Huddling together is good for keeping warm especially if someone is showing signs of exposure or hypothermia which is when you have a below normal body temperature which can be dangerous. If this happens you should get into a sleeping bag with them.

Quick think

Snakes are one of the dangers that you should be ready for when hiking or camping in the Australian bush. How much do you know already about snakes? Are the following true or false?

1 In general, a large snake is more dangerous than a small snake because it can deliver more venom.

____

2 You are more likely to be bitten by a dog than a snake. ____________________

3 In Australia, there are about 20 known deaths of snakebite each year. ____________________

4 Most people who die from snakebite are female. ____________________

5 Many cases of snakebite have been associated with alcohol intoxication (being drunk). ____________________

6 If someone is bitten by a snake, you should apply firm pressure over the bitten area and immobilise the limb. ____________________

7 You should not try to cut or suck out the venom. ____________________

8 You should wash the bitten area. ____________________

*P*roofreading

Punctuate this paragraph using full stops and commas.

Conserving water is essential use creek water for washing up but do not wash in the creek as food residue can harm the creatures that inhabit it think about what your water needs are do not drink too much water sip it at regular intervals rather than drinking it in large quantities at less frequent intervals your body will absorb it better if you must use creek water boil it or bring a couple of water-purifying tablets they taste awful but will do the job.

Writing paragraphs and whole texts

1 These action verbs are missing from the instructions below. Where do they belong?

provide, use, avoid, lay out, try, expose, make, indicate, make

Air searches for lost persons

Light aircraft are an important aid in searches for lost persons in the Australian bush. To **a** ______________ misunderstanding only **b** ______________ the ground-to-air code described below.

I	require doctor	II	require medical supplies	F	require food and water
Y	yes	N	no	LL	all well
↑	proceeding in this direction	K	indicate direction to proceed	NN	nothing found continuing search
JL	not understood				

Do not **c** ______________ any signals to aircraft unless in distress or searching. The pilot will indicate that ground signals have been seen and understood by rocking the aircraft from side to side. He/she will **d** ______________ that the signals have been seen but not understood by making complete right-hand circuits. **e** ______________ these symbols exactly as shown by using brightly coloured ground sheets, clothing, sleeping bags or wood. **f** ______________ as great a colour contrast as possible between the material used for the symbol and the ground. **g** ______________ the symbols 2.5 metres in length or more. **h** ______________ the ground if it is snowing.

In addition to using these symbols, **i** ______________ to attract attention by means of smoke signals, flares, mirrors or movement.

2 Many instructions include 'if' clauses, e.g. *If any signs of illness are apparent, the whole party should immediately pitch tents* ... Complete these instructions by using one of the 'if' clauses below.

- If there is a heavy storm
- If you see a snake
- If you are considering a hike in the remote wilderness
- If there is lightning
- If you've planned a long hike for the weekend but the forecast is for mid-30s temperatures

a ______________________________,

then go to the movies and do it next weekend.

b ______________________________,

try to find shelter under a rock or in a cave.

c ______________________________,

avoid isolated trees and powerlines.

d ______________________________,

consider buying a short-wave radio or a mobile phone.

e ______________________________,

the safest thing to do is avoid it.

3 Follow these steps to write a set of instructions for some activity or situation you are familiar with.

- Begin with a statement of the purpose of your instructions.
- Break up the instructions into clear, small steps.
- Include enough detail so that someone could actually use your instructions.
- Include comments where necessary on the importance or usefulness of what you are saying.
- Use headings where it is necessary to break your instructions into stages.

Here are some outdoor topics you might like to try:

putting up a tent, packing a rucksack or backpack, mouth-to-mouth resuscitation, avoiding sunburn, making a campfire.

Use the space below for notes or drafting.

____

____

____

____

____

____

____

____

____

____

____

CHAPTER 5

Book report

STRUCTURE

title and/or opening sentence, which identifies title and author (and perhaps type of book)

a plot summary organised chronologically

should be written with the expectation that the reader has not read the book

only main events of plot and a few plot details

broad overview of sections or plot

comment on aspects of author's writing style or technique

description of main characters

concludes with opinion of book and usually a recommendation to other readers

Tomorrow, When the War Began by John Marsden

This fantastic novel is about seven teenagers who go on a hike for a week to a secluded wilderness called Hell, 'a cauldron of boulders and trees and blackberries and feral dogs and wombats and undergrowth'. When the group return home, they discover that their country has been invaded. Their families have been taken prisoner and their town is in chaos. After a series of terrifying adventures including an outrageous rescue of one group member in a bulldozer, they retreat to Hell for safety reasons. While there, the group work out their options. They decide that they will make their base in Hell but that they will not just hide. They will try to do something for their country and fight against the enemy.

The story is told from the point of view of Ellie, one of the teenagers. She has been chosen by the group as the one who should record what has happened. Her story illustrates how seven normal teenagers can change from being innocent outback high school students to courageous heroes fighting for their country. Desperate and extraordinary events are described one minute and normal teenage worries and emotions the next. For example, Ellie is thinking about boys and love at the same time as she is worrying about whether her parents are alive and working out ways to survive.

The main characters are Ellie, Lee, Fi, Corrie, Kevin, Robyn and Homer, and a boy named Chris who they find in hiding later on in their adventures. Ellie describes each of the teenage characters quite early in the book, but makes a point of saying that that was 'the way they were then—or the way I thought they were, because of course they've changed, and my knowledge of them has changed'. By the end of the book, this change is very great. They have all grown in each other's eyes and learned a great deal about war, about life and death, and about themselves.

Tomorrow, When the War Began is a tense, exciting and frighteningly realistic story, the first of a seven-part series. Although written in 1993 the book is still included in most lists of the best teen fiction ever—and rightly so in my opinion. I found it 'unputdownable' —literally. In fact I read it in one day. I would recommend it to everyone—both adolescents and adults. It is one of Marsden's best.

Sally Dennis

LANGUAGE FEATURES

can be informal, everyday language

may be quotations from the book to illustrate a point or to give example of writer's style

chronological linking words and phrases, e.g. 'after', 'while'

present or past tense to retell the story

consistent use of whatever tense is chosen

subjective language (speaking from own point of view)

Comprehension

If a book report is well written, you should be able to understand it even if you have not read the book. The writer will give enough information about the plot and characters for you to appreciate his or her comments and opinions.

1 If we were using a star rating system (five stars being the best), how many stars do you think this writer would give *Tomorrow, When the War Began*? ______________________________

2 On the basis of the report, put these events into the order in which they happened in the book:

_____ **a** group of teenagers make base in Hell
_____ **b** group of teenagers go on a hike to Hell
_____ **c** group of teenagers fight the enemy
_____ **d** country is invaded
_____ **e** group of teenagers rescue one of their members in a bulldozer

3 Are the following true or false, based on information in the report?

a The teenagers live in a country town. ______________________________

b The teenagers decide to surrender, but then change their minds. ______________________________

c Only one of the teenagers writes the story of their adventures. ______________________________

d The writer of the report says she has read all the series. ______________________________

4 What particular aspect of the characters is discussed? Underline the correct answer.

a how many main characters there are
b how interesting they all were
c how they changed during their experiences

5 If you have read this book, do you agree with this reviewer? Why or why not? If you have not read the book, would you now like to? Why or why not? (one or two sentences)

____

Writing skills

Book reports do not always follow the same structure, but like all good writing they need to be **organised into paragraphs**. In general, each paragraph will be about one particular aspect of the book (characters, plot, style, point of view).

1 These sentences are missing from the report. Mark an ✗ in the text to show where you think they belong. Doing this task will make you more aware of its good organisation.

a *The only other characters in the novel are the enemy soldiers and the parents of the teenagers who are held in captivity.*
b *I cannot remember the last time I did this.*
c *They can hide, they can surrender, or they can fight.*
d *Because of this, the book is like a diary.*

2 One interesting way to begin a book report is to use a quotation that gives the reader a sense of the book's content or style. Which of the following quotations from the book would you use to begin this report, and why? There is more than one possibility.

a *But in front of me came another noise: the unmistakable sound of a bolt being drawn back in a breech, then slid forward to cock the rifle.*

b *Huge granite blocks that look like they were chucked there in random order by some drunken giant, back in the Stone Age.*

c *It's only half an hour since someone—Robyn I think—said we should write everything down, and it's only twenty-nine minutes since I got chosen ...*

d *That was the first moment at which I started to realise what true courage was.*

The **present tense** is usually used to retell the story in a book report or review for two reasons. First, the book exists in the present time—so in a way the events are happening now. Secondly, the present tense can make any telling of events more immediate and exciting.

3 The report uses the present tense to retell the story, but past tense forms and the future tense may be used where there is a need to distinguish between two points in time. Look at the first and second paragraphs only.

a Underline all the verbs (e.g. *is, go, return*).

b Then circle those that are in the past or the future tense.

c Look at the remainder of the report. Which tenses are used and why?

4 List all the words the report writer uses to describe her reaction to the book.

5 What does 'unputdownable' mean?

Vocabulary

secluded	**cauldron**	**boulders**	**feral**	**invaded**
chaos	**terrifying**	**outrageous**	**rescue**	**retreat**
options	**decide**	**illustrates**	**innocent**	**courageous**
desperate	**extraordinary**	**tense**	**literally**	**recommend**

Breaking words into sound chunks (called **syllables**) can help you to spell them, because all words have at least one letter for each syllable you hear. In the list above *tense* has one syllable, *caul-dron* has two, and *inn-o-cent* has three.

Write out all the words in the list, breaking them up into syllables in the same way. Then learn them using the Look, Cover, Write, Check method.

Focus on punctuation

Quotation marks

We use **quotation marks** '...' in two main ways:

- to enclose the title of a published work (e.g. a book, film, play, newspaper)
- to enclose the exact words that someone else has written or said.

Note:

- We usually use capital letters for the main words in a title, though writers vary about which words they capitalise.
- You may use single or double quotation marks. Note that single quotation marks are used in this book.
- Use italics instead of quotation marks for titles of published works if you are typing.

1 Use quotation marks where needed in these sentences.

a Have you read the sequel to The Hitch Hiker's Guide to the Galaxy?

b A Midsummer Night's Dream is my favourite Shakespearean play.

c The last lines of Tomorrow, When the War Began were I just hope we can survive.

d I read a review of that film in The Australian and decided not to see it.

e The school's performance of West Side Story was the best I've seen anywhere.

2 Tick the sentence below that shows the correct use of quotation marks.

a George Orwell's '1984' begins: It was a bright cold day in April and the clocks were striking thirteen.

b George Orwell's 1984 begins: 'It was a bright cold day in April and the clocks were striking thirteen.'

c George Orwell's '1984' begins: 'It was a bright cold day in April and the clocks were striking thirteen.

d George Orwell's '1984' begins: 'It was a bright cold day in April and the clocks were striking thirteen.'

Select a word

Choose words from the vocabulary list that mean the same as these words.

1 exactly, actually, not exaggerated ____________________

2 choices ____________________

3 complete confusion ____________________

4 large kettle or cooking pot ____________________

5 wild, untamed ____________________

6 withdraw from a dangerous situation ____________________

7 shows ____________________

8 isolated ____________________

Grammar

Clauses and complex sentences

- Remember: a **clause** is the basic unit of meaning.
- Many sentences consist of more than one clause.
- Some of these have clauses of equal importance (**compound sentences**).
- Others have one clause that is the important 'stand-alone' clause (the **main** or **independent** clause) and another less important clause (a **dependent** or **subordinate** clause) that depends for meaning on the main clause. We call these **complex** sentences.

- In the sentences below the main clause is underlined.

  Ellie is chosen as the diary writer because she is the best at English.

  When the group return home, they make a dreadful discovery.
- We link main clauses to dependent clauses with **conjunctions** such as:

  because, as, since, after, when, in order that, so that, if, although, even though, unless, whereas, as soon as, until, before, as if, as long as, whenever, where, wherever, whether
- Note: a sentence may have more than one dependent clause or more than one independent clause.

1 Underline the main clause in these sentences, and circle the conjunctions, e.g.
(While) the group are in Hell, their town is invaded by another country.

a When they get back, their parents have been taken hostage.

b The small group decide to go back to town, even though they are terrified.

c The book only took me one day to read, because I simply could not put it down.

d You really want to read the next book as soon as you finish this one.

e You should give this book a go, despite what you may have heard.

f If you want non-stop action thrills, this is a brilliant choice.

2 Choose an appropriate conjunction from the list above to complete these complex sentences. There may be more than one possible answer.

a My friends told me all about it ____________________ I read it.

b I thoroughly enjoyed it, ____________________ the ending was a little disappointing.

c ____________________ my mother bought this book for me, I began to read it.

d I did not stop reading it ____________________ I got to the end.

e I still cry ____________________ I think of that sad, sad book.

f I'd advise you not to read this book ____________________ you have locked all the doors and windows.

3 Match the main clauses on the left and the dependent clauses on the right so that they make sense. (Write the letters and numerals on the line below.) Note: we often separate main clauses and dependent clauses with a comma. Think about which sentences below would need a comma.

a The book will appeal to all ages

b I will definitely be buying the next book in the series

c You'll enjoy this novel immensely

d This book is futuristic fantasy

e The author writes

i as if he is really there in the action

ii whereas the author's last book was set in a real time and place

iii although it is written mainly for young adults

iv as long as you love a bit of romance

v as soon as it comes out

Word study

Use your dictionary to group the words and expressions that have similar meanings:

authentic, action-packed, comic, believable, suspenseful, tragic, tense, glued to, moving, taut, true-to-life, engrossing, hilarious, hooked, realistic, accurate, lively, not a dull moment, humorous, heart-breaking, adventure-filled, mysterious, gripped, witty

Evaluating other people's writing

What is wrong with the student's book report below? Mark at least five things in the report that could be improved, e.g.

- content
- vocabulary and grammar
- organisation of ideas
- punctuation

This book was simply amazing. I have read it so many times now and I still think it is good. The writer, John Marsden, is brilliant. I can't really explain why I like it so much but I guess it is because so much happens in it and I like the characters. Most kids know the story so I'll only mention the main things. This group of kids goes on a hike to the bush to a place called Hell. They have a great time but when they get back the town has been invaded. They go back to Hell first they have some amazing adventures. Especially where they rescue Lee in the bulldozer. That was one of the best bits. I liked all the characters. I have read most of the other books in the series too. My mum even liked this book, which is pretty amazing.

Quick think

Complete this crossword with words you might find in a book report. Clues are over the page.

Across

6 the main good characters (usually brave and strong)

9 clever, outstanding

11 the reader is in ______________________ the whole time

14 a crime story is often called a ______________ if it is very scary

15 true-to-life

16 the people in a story or play

Down

1 where and when the story happens

2 a book-length story

3 a long adjective which means 'I could not stop reading this book'

4 the things that happen in a story

5 a similar word to 'hooked' or 'glued to'

7 the way a writer writes

8 the adjective from 'mystery'

10 another word for 'writer'

12 extremely sad

13 suggest as being good

Proofreading

Put full stops and commas where needed in this paragraph from a student's book report.

In *Z for Zachariah* by Robert O'Brien Ann Burden appears to be the lone survivor after a nuclear holocaust she sees a column of smoke over the mountains coming closer each evening in fright she moves to a cave and then watches another survivor come over the hill it is a man by the name of Mr John Loomis after recovering from a deadly illness Mr Loomis seems to be threatening Ann's solitary life in the green valley Ann must decide whether Mr Loomis is a friend or enemy she must decide if the kind man she first knew has turned into a crazed maniac

Writing paragraphs and whole texts

It can be difficult to write about a book plot in one paragraph. You have to make choices about what, and about how much, you will include, and then be clear about the order in which things happened. The next two activities will help you focus on the importance of choice and order.

1 Number these sentences from this plot summary in an order that makes the best sense (from a book report about *The Silver Crown* by Robert O'Brien).

____ **a** When she returns she finds that something disastrous has happened to her family.

____ **b** So she takes her priceless possession and a little money with her and begins the long journey to her aunt's house.

____ **c** Ellen wakes up on the morning of her birthday with a silver crown on her pillow.

____ **d** Along the way, Ellen encounters some very menacing people and situations.

____ **e** The only person she knows and trusts is Aunt Sarah who lives 400 miles away.

____ **f** She places it on her head and tiptoes out for an early morning walk.

2 Think of a short and simple children's fairytale that you know well (for example, 'Little Red Riding Hood'). Make some brief notes on your own paper about the main things that happen in the story. Then decide which points would be important to tell someone else if they had never read the story. Now convert your plot summary points into a short paragraph.

____

____

3 When writing a book report, you should try as much as possible to give reasons for any opinion you express. For example, you should not just say *The book is interesting*, but you could say, for example, *The book is interesting because of the way it combines real-life and fantasy*. Match these opinions to the reasons given (a–e) and then complete the opinions (f–g) with possible reasons.

a	I liked the characters	**i**	because of the predictable characters and plot
b	The book was so thrilling	**ii**	—action, romance, suspense and adventure.
c	The book is a great read	**iii**	because it is action-packed as well as thought-provoking.
d	I did not like the book at all,	**iv**	because they were amusing and unusual.
e	This series has it all	**v**	that I convinced my parents to read it.

f I love this book ______________________________

g I thought it an excellent book ______________________________

h He is my favourite character______________________________

4 Write a report on a book you have read, using your own paper. Follow these steps:

- Give the title of the book and the author and say something about the type of book (and perhaps your overall reaction).
- Summarise the plot focusing on the main events only. Include one or two points of detail to convey a sense of the writer's style. Use quotation marks for any exact words from the book. Remember that you are writing this for someone who has not read the book.
- Say something about one or two of the main characters or about an interesting minor character.
- Give your opinion of the book, commenting on the writer's style, the characters, the setting, the plot or other aspects of interest. Be honest and comment on both the positive and negative.

CHAPTER 6

Description of a scene

Write a description of a crowd scene you have experienced, e.g. concert, sports game or street crowd.

STRUCTURE

overall structure reflects text purpose—to describe a scene

orientation to scene by reference to action, location, time etc.

different aspects of the scene, e.g. the people, the stadium, the players

only some details included—selection of detail to suit writing purpose, e.g. to give a sense of mood, to amuse etc.

sometimes a comment or evaluation of the scene or elements

conclusion, which brings the description to an end, e.g. by returning to the beginning in some way

The game

'GIIIRD-LAA, GIIIRD-LAA, GIIIRD-LAA, GIIIRD-LAA.' 'Whumpf.' And it flies off into the sparkling sun, spinning towards the goalposts. But it's gone too far and they're up. Pimply teenagers, weather-beaten old men, women, kids—all screeching fanatics—all on their feet cheering and clapping. They've done their job. Played their part in the weekly ritual. With their jeering they've successfully put a young player off his game and saved their team two valuable points.

The whistle blows and the hard fought conflict is on again. Individual differences are forgotten under the colours of the teams. Old are young, meek are strong, all are united. One team battles it out against the other in the grandstand. It's a match of wit and passion, of insults and physical threats, but curiously it rarely comes to blows.

On the grassy hill the smell of beer and chips overwhelms. No-one can tell who is going for whom. All that matters is that you are yelling your lungs out: 'Are yer blind or sumthin?' 'Where'd yer learn ta ref?', 'Offside? OFFSIDE? Ya gotta be kidding', 'Get your rule book out ref'.

An old lady leaps from her wheelchair, waving her blanket in the air as her favourite player goes crashing over the line. She can barely see the scoreboard through her inch-thick glasses, but she knows she's in front and there's not long till the full-time hooter.

A group of boys come sprinting past her on their way to the goalposts, desperate to touch the ball as it zooms through the uprights. Leaping over fans, scattering bags, chip cartons and other debris as they go. They burn with the idea. Oh, to touch that ball.

A father whisks a bundle away as they thunder past and holds it high. It's almost unrecognisable as a baby girl under the layers of jersey, beanie, scarf and other team gear. She looks more like a flag. Her father seems to think so too and waves her in the air as number 12 swings his foot. The ball sails high again and the flags are up.

This time the hecklers don't get to him and he grabs back the two points he lost to them earlier. The stadium is ringing with his name as his two precious points are posted on the scoreboard. This time it is his own supporters singing his name. 'Girdler, Girdler, Girdler.'

William McLean

LANGUAGE FEATURES

opening words, which instantly capture reader's interest

pronouns to refer to people and things

descriptive language to create images in reader's mind—visual, sound etc.

writer here writes as if he is an outsider looking in and uses third, person ('they're', 'no-one'), not first person ('I', 'we're', 'we' (can't))

not always complete sentences—words and phrases used to create impact

many action verbs, e.g. 'swings', 'grabs'

consistent use of whatever tense is chosen—here present tense is used to make scene seem closer

Comprehension

A good description of a scene allows you as the reader to visualise what is going on, even if you have never witnessed such a scene yourself. You can see it, hear it, feel it and sometimes even smell or taste it. Reading this text, you can actually feel the movement and the excitement of the game and the whole crowd.

1 What scene is the writer describing? Underline the correct answer.

a a football game **b** an athletics competition **c** a basketball game

d Is the focus mainly on the game itself or on the people watching the game?

____

2 Underline the words that tell you what scene the writer is describing.

3 What does the crowd do at the beginning of the description? Underline the correct answer.

a Make the opposition goal kicker miss the goal. **b** Encourage their goal kicker to get the goal.

c Cheer the goal kicker for kicking a goal successfully.

4 What does the writer mean when he says: *Individual differences are forgotten under the colours of the team*? Underline the correct answer.

a The supporters of the two teams forget they are on opposite sides once the game begins.

b The supporters of a team are all equal at the game regardless of their backgrounds.

5 Why does the writer think that it is curious that *it rarely comes to blows?* _______________

____

6 Which sentence in paragraph 3 suggests that the writer is part of the crowd he describes?

____

Writing skills

1 There are many action verbs in 'The game' that help to create an interesting picture of the scene. Underline as many as you can find.

2 Write down the interesting verbs used instead of the following:

a falling (para 4) _______________

b running (para 5) _______________

c goes (para 5) _______________

d are filled with (para 5) _______________

e shifts (para 6) _______________

f run (para 6) _______________

3 The images in the text relate to all five senses: vision, sound, smell, touch, taste. Which two types of images are used most? Write down some examples of each.

____

____

____

When writing descriptions, you usually need to refer to many people and things, and to keep it clear to whom you are referring. You could use names or specific nouns throughout (e.g. the old lady did this, the old lady did that, then the old lady did ...), but this will be very boring. A good use of **pronouns** such as *he*, *she*, *they* or *it* help you to avoid this problem. However, you need to use them very well or your reader will get lost.

4 The writer uses pronouns such as *he, they, it* to refer to people and things in the text. What do the pronouns in italics refer to in the text?

a And *it* flies off into the sparkling sun ... ______

b *They've* done their job. ______

c ... curiously *it* rarely comes to blows. ______

d A group of boys come sprinting past *her* on their way ...______

e A father whisks a bundle away as *they* thunder past and holds it high. ______

f This time the hecklers don't get to *him* ... ______

5 The writer manages to cover a whole stadium of people and the actions of the whole crowd in seven paragraphs. He does this by swiftly moving from one aspect of the scene to another. Look back at the text and write down the focus of each paragraph. For example, paragraph one focuses on the crowd jeering at the player attempting to kick a goal.

Para 2 ______

Para 3 ______

Para 4 ______

Para 5 ______

Para 6 ______

What does the writer do in the last paragraph to bring the description full circle?

______

______

6 The writer wrote these sentences in the original draft. Circle the sentences in the text that replaced them and say why he changed them.

a *An old lady leaps from her wheelchair in joy along with the screaming fans waving her blanket in the air as her favourite player goes crashing over the line.*

b *To touch the ball that their idol has held has been a dream for all of them for a long time.*

c *There are all sorts of people there—young and old, male and female.*

d *This time the hecklers didn't get to him and he has grabbed back the two points he lost to them earlier.*

e *The final score was 14 all.*

Vocabulary

sparkling	**weather-beaten**	**screeching**	**fanatics**	**ritual**
jeering	**successfully**	**valuable**	**conflict**	**meek**
passion	**overwhelms**	**favourite**	**barely**	**desperate**
scattering	**debris**	**whisks**	**unrecognisable**	**hecklers**

Learn the words using the Look, Cover, Write, Check method.

Focus on punctuation

Apostrophes

We use apostrophes for two purposes:

- to show that we have left out a letter (**apostrophe of omission**), e.g. *I'll (I will), she's (she is* or *she has), they've (they have), it's (it is* or *it has)*
- to show a relationship of ownership between two nouns (**apostrophe of possession**), e.g. *the crowd's jeers, the team's colours, the supporters' cries*

  (See Chapter 7 for more on apostrophe of possession.)

The words *it's* and *its* confuse many writers.

- *it's* means *it is* or *it has*, e.g. *It's raining.* **You only write** it's **if you mean** it is **or** it has.
- *its* is a pronoun. It does not use an apostrophe even though it shows possession, e.g. *The dog has lost its tail.*

Note: You don't need an apostrophe just to show a plural, e.g.
The boys came sprinting past. NOT *The boys' came sprinting past.*
AND NOT *The boy's came sprinting past.*
(*boys* is a simple plural—it is not indicating possession of anything.)

1 Look back at the text 'The game' and underline all words that use an apostrophe.

2 For each word, decide if it is the apostrophe of omission or possession that is used.

____

3 Complete the sentences below with *it's* or *its*.

a ______________ a very exciting game.

b The crowd lost ______________ enthusiasm very quickly.

c The team seemed to lose ______________ way after the second half.

d The game is almost over but ______________ still nil-all.

4 Tick the sentence that is correctly punctuated with apostrophes.

a The Tigers' fans gathered excitedly to watch their team's last game.

b The Tigers' fan's gathered excitedly to watch their team's last game.

c The Tiger's fans gathered excitedly to watch their teams last game.

d The Tigers' fans gathered excitedly to watch their teams' last game.

e The Tiger's fans gathered excitedly to watch their team's last game.

Select a word

Choose words from the vocabulary list that mean the same as these words.

1 rubbish ______________

2 only just ______________

3 overcomes, overpowers ______________

4 humble, quiet ______________

5 without much hope ______________

6 mocking, insulting ______________

7 set, often repeated procedure ______________

8 people who harass or bother a performer ______________

Grammar

Phrases

- A **phrase** is a group of words that adds meaning to a sentence about, for example, when, where, why, and how, e.g.
  into the sparkling sun, with their jeering, till the full-time hooter, like a flag
- A **phrase** differs from a **clause** in that it does not contain a complete verb, e.g.
  The goalie placed the ball with care. ('with care' is a phrase)
  The goalie placed the ball as the crowd waited. ('as the crowd waited' is a clause)
- Phrases add detail to the information or idea in a sentence or clause, so they are useful in descriptive writing.
- Many phrases begin with a preposition (e.g. *under, until, near, with, to, among, between, against, within, since, through, during, over, in front of, about*).

1 Underline the phrases in these sentences. (There many be more than one in each.)
e.g. *The players leapt in the air with excitement.*

a Thousands fill the stadium every weekend.
b They play like madmen for a full eighty minutes.
c When the hooter went, a little old man near me cried.
d Mud spatters onto the closest spectators.
e The crowd rose to their feet as one.

2 Complete these sentences that phrases that add detail about when, where, why or how.

a Kids run ______________________________, as the full-time hooter sounds.
b Silence falls ______________________________, as he takes the kick.
c The ball flies ______________________________.
d The noise ______________________________ gradually increases.

Word study

The writer of 'The game' uses a number of everyday expressions associated with sport.

1 Find these expressions in the text and look at how they are used:

put a player off his game (paragraph 1); *battles it out* (paragraph 2); *it comes to blows* (paragraph 2); *who is going for whom* (paragraph 3); *yell your lungs out* (paragraph 3); *don't get to him* (last paragraph)

2 What do these sporting expressions mean?

a win hands down ______________________________
b thrash the opposition ______________________________
c the team folded ______________________________
d the cheers lifted the rafters ______________________________
e he's a sore loser ______________________________
f turn the game around ______________________________
g stadium was filled to the rafters ______________________________
h the crowd erupted ______________________________
i play hard ______________________________
j give the game your all ______________________________
k a dream run ______________________________

Evaluating other people's writing

What is wrong with the student's description below? Mark at least five things that could be improved, e.g.

- the orientation to the scene
- the conclusion
- the grammar and punctuation
- the level of detail
- the language used to create images

There are about one hundred people standing on the platform this morning. They don't seem too happy to be there. I suppose they do not want to go to work or school and would rather be still lying in bed. I know I would, many of them are schoolchildren. The younger ones at least are cheerful and bright, they laugh and talk with each other. Some men and women wait patiently for the train to come in. They look cold. Some of them are reading newspapers. Others just look along the line to see if the train is coming. Some mornings the train is late. It looks like it might be late today too. People start looking at their watches. At last it comes. They look happy now. They'll be on time. I get on the train with them and find a seat.

Quick think

The words down the side of the page describe the sounds people might make at a sports game:

Check the meanings of those words above that you do not know. Then find as many as you can in the wordsearch below.

groan
screech
jeer
cheer
moan
howl
roar
shriek
squeal
yell
yowl
wail
sigh
hoot
holler
shout
barrack
boo
hiss

X	A	R	H	O	O	T	E	E	F	O	N	U	S
F	T	R	O	O	P	T	H	X	Y	P	T	E	I
E	A	K	W	A	I	L	R	J	E	E	R	Z	G
C	A	N	L	T	E	R	R	E	Z	O	U	N	H
H	L	E	M	R	O	S	C	A	N	R	S	E	A
E	D	E	S	P	S	H	O	U	T	H	O	C	R
E	A	B	C	A	N	D	O	H	O	M	E	A	A
R	V	A	L	B	A	R	R	A	C	K	U	A	R
B	A	R	L	Y	K	E	A	M	Z	M	A	N	Y
C	O	M	S	C	R	E	E	C	H	E	S	T	O
B	H	E	H	S	E	L	B	E	S	O	N	T	O
O	L	E	R	D	A	R	N	O	M	O	A	N	F
O	P	S	I	F	A	H	O	L	L	E	R	D	S
D	R	E	E	S	S	S	T	O	N	D	E	N	Q
F	G	R	K	A	G	E	T	Y	O	W	L	N	U
C	H	R	E	C	K	O	T	J	E	L	M	O	E
O	N	E	O	Z	O	M	E	D	R	L	E	A	A
R	Y	L	O	A	O	K	S	M	I	G	L	H	L
H	I	S	S	T	N	L	A	S	P	A	P	E	R

Proofreading

Correct these spellings. Check your corrections against the chapter vocabulary list.

sparkleing	wether-beaten	ritule	jering	sucesfully
valueable	meak	pasion	overwelms	favrite
barly	desperite	scatering	wisks	unreconisable

Writing paragraphs and whole texts

1 In creative writing, it is common to use short groups of words instead of full sentences to create images. Complete this crowd description with the groups of words from the box.

- Good news or bad news?
- Bit chilly this morning.
- Grey faces.
- Silence shattered.
- Two down and two to go.
- Lollies, crisps, even hot chips.

a ______________________ A grey morning. Silence at the station as they wait for the 6.42. What day is it? Wednesday. **b** ______________________

Men, young and not so young. In suits or jackets of varying dark hues—brown, black and, yes, grey. Most carry laptops in special little bags. They'll be able to get an hour's work in before they even get to the city. Many are on their phones. Talking into the air or texting urgently. It's early, so there are clusters here and there of men in boots, sweaters and high-vis vests. They too are engrossed in their phones.

The women look perkier. More colourful too, though there are gloomy suits among them as well. They pull their jackets around them as the wind blows in from the west.

c ______________________

Here come the kids. **d** ______________________ They gallop down the stairs, three at a time. Their energy leaves the adults gaping. It's so early. The kids wear various combinations of school colours. Blue and green checks here, maroon blazers there. Most are chomping away on some food or other. **e** ______________________ How can they? It's so early. The loudspeaker crackles. The station master calls the crowd to attention.

f ______________________ 'The 6.42 is running fifteen minutes late. We apologise for any inconvenience.' A collective groan goes up. The wind blows.

2 Write a description of a crowd scene you have experienced, e.g. at school, church, a sporting event or party. Close your eyes and imagine you are there. What can you see? What can you hear? What can you smell? Is there any particularly interesting detail?

- Open your eyes and think about these questions.
  What aspects of the scene would you include? e.g. people, buildings, actions
  Which sense would you mainly focus on in building your image of the scene? e.g. sight, sound
  Which tense would best suit your description?
  Will you be in the scene yourself (and so talk about *I* or *we*) or will you write it as if you are an outsider looking in (and use only *they*, *it*, *he*, *she*)?
  How will you introduce your scene? How will you organise the images and ideas?
- Now quickly jot down some ideas from your reflection. Don't worry about whole sentences—a single word or a short phrase may do to remind you of an interesting part of the scene. Jot down as much as you can in the space opposite.

- Start writing your draft. Don't try to cover everything. Select only the most interesting things, and use images that your readers will be able to relate to, using the space below as needed.

CHAPTER 7

Short story

STRUCTURE

overall structure reflects text purpose—to tell a story that engages and entertains the reader

the orientation to subject of story—by reference to subject and/or by reference to location, time, situation etc.

the 'complication'—unfolding of the main events of story—leading up to critical event or problem

the 'resolution' or conclusion—crisis or problem is wholly or partly resolved

the resolution stage contains a number of paragraphs as the story moves towards its final conclusion

last paragraph dramatically rounds off the story, making a comment of a kind on the events related

The journey

Stumbling, he made his way forward, the blistering wind tearing into him. Two days in weather like this had tempted him beyond measure to turn tail and go back the way he had come.

But he had something to prove. All his life he had followed in his father's famous footsteps, forever being compared to him and found wanting. His father, the fearless explorer and adventurer. Whatever he had decided to do, his father had already done, and done better. In an attempt to break free of his father's shadow, he had gone where his father had never been. Antarctica, no man's land, the land of death.

He shivered, partly from the cold and partly from the knowledge of what lay ahead. He plodded on. The pack he carried began to weigh him down. He had never felt so tired. Doggedly, he persisted, his sharp eyes hunting for shelter from the relentless winds. He had found shelter in caves the first two nights, but tonight it seemed he was doomed to spend the night in his small tent. He groaned. The tent was no protection from the frigidity of the air.

Once the tent was up and a meagre dinner eaten, he settled down to sleep with his dogs by his side—his lone, faithful companions. Oblivion claimed him in less than a minute.

The next day progressed reasonably well. He trudged onwards, his once sharp vision blurring from the endless glare of the sun. Perhaps it was because of this that he failed to notice the thinning of the ice under his feet.

When the ice began to crack it came as a complete surprise. Panic and terror gave way quickly to the strength of his will. He set to work, freeing his dogs from their harnesses so they could escape. He abandoned his backpack and began running for his life, the ice falling behind him into freezing cold water. He knew that if he was to fall into that water, he would die. Now the falling ice was catching him. He saw that he would not make it.

It was in that moment that he knew. He reflected upon his folly. How foolish to want to be greater than his father. How foolish to think that what others thought of him was important. And lastly, how foolish to think that man could conquer nature.

The dogs looked back as they saw their master go down. In unison, they howled their grief and sorrow. The wind carried the sounds of their howls for miles in all directions.

Kim Ung

LANGUAGE FEATURES

opening words that instantly capture reader interest

third person ('he') but many stories in first person ('I')

not always complete sentences—words and phrases used for impact

varied sentence length

past tense to tell story

descriptive language to create images in reader's mind, e.g. 'trudged'

action verbs

pronouns to refer backwards and forwards to people and things

Comprehension

Short stories aim to do more than tell us what happened. They generally aim to engage us—to entertain or amuse us, to make us think about certain aspects of the life or the world, or to move us emotionally. To do this, however, they need to be written in a way that we can understand.

1 Tick which of the themes below appear in the story.

old age ______ loneliness ______ youth ______ nature ______

illness ______ self-knowledge ______ violence ______ relationships ______ death ______

2 Underline one phrase or sentence from the story that reflects each theme you selected. Which theme do you think is most important?

____

3 Underline which of the following sentences below best sums up the story.

a The story is about a man who wants to prove he is better than his father.

b The story is about a man who goes alone to Antarctica.

c The story is about a man who dies during an Antarctic adventure.

4 Where would you add these sentences?

a Besides, it would take him hours to set it up in gales of this magnitude. ______________

b Their body warmth would perhaps make sleeping a little easier. ______________

c The scenery was the same as the previous days. ______________

5 Are the following true or false?

a The man's father was an explorer. ______________

b The man was part of an expedition team. ______________

c The man did not notice the thinning of the ice till it was too late. ______________

d The dogs went down into the ice with the man. ______________

6 The title of the story has two possible meanings. What do you think they are?

____

Writing skills

Many stories do not begin by telling us everything we need to know. The writer often gives us just enough to go on with. We have to fill in the details in our heads as we read on. Most **orientations** (first paragraphs) do, however, tell us something about the subject and the setting.

1 Underline which of the following details we know after reading the orientation to 'The journey' (first two paragraphs).

a that the subject of the story is a young man

b the subject's name

c where the story's action takes place

d when the story's action takes place

e something interesting or special about the subject

2 Writers need to use effective descriptive language to create images in their readers' minds, but it is important not to overload the reader with descriptive language. Read the story again and underline the words this writer has used to create effective images of the story subject and the scene.

3 The **complication** of a story is where the writer describes the main events, usually leading up to one critical event or problem. Put these events of the complication into the order in which they occur:

a the ice began to crack ______
b he woke up ______
c he went to sleep ______
d he was cold and tired ______
e he began walking again ______
f he put up his tent ______
g he ran for his life ______
h he ate his meal ______
i he looked for shelter ______
j he let his dogs go ______

4 Does the ending of the story resolve the story completely—that is, tell you exactly what happened to the man and his dogs? Did you like this ending or not, and why?

____

____

Vocabulary

blistering	**wanting**	**shivered**	**plodded**	**doggedly**
persisted	**relentless**	**doomed**	**frigidity**	**meagre**
lone	**companions**	**oblivion**	**trudged**	**blurring**
abandoned	**reflected**	**folly**	**conquer**	**unison**

One-syllable words with a short vowel sound must double the final letter before adding an *~ed*, or *~ing* (or any other ending beginning with a vowel) in order to keep the short vowel sound, e.g. *plod—plodded, dog—dogged* (*blur* does not, strictly speaking, have a short vowel sound but *~ur* words double anyway).

With words of more than one syllable, if the last syllable has only one vowel, we double the last consonant before adding endings beginning with a vowel, e.g. *regretted, committing, forgotten.*

1 Add *~ed* and *~ing* to these words:

a thin **b** snap **c** wrap **d** plan **e** step

____

2 Learn the words in the list using the Look, Cover, Write, Check method.

3 In which of the following sentences is the spelling completely correct?

a The wind whiped their faces and tugged at their clothes but the climbers could not be detered from their important goal.

b The wind whipped their faces and tugged at their clothes but the climbers could not be deterred from their important goal.

c The wind whipped their faces and tugged at their clothes but the climbers could not be detered from their important goal.

d The wind whipped their faces and tuged at their clothes but the climbers could not be deterred from their important goal.

Focus on punctuation

Apostrophe of possession

- The **apostrophe of possession** often troubles writers. Look at these examples:
  this father's footsteps (the footsteps of his father)
  the dogs' food (the food of the dogs)
  the men's campsite (the campsite of the men)

- In each case the apostrophe shows a relationship of ownership or possession between two nouns (people or things).
- In every case, the apostrophe goes immediately after the 'owner' or 'possessor' (the person or thing who 'owns' the noun that follows it).
- When you are deciding where to put the apostrophe ask yourself 'Who is the owner?'; write the word, and immediately put the apostrophe after it. This is the only rule you have to remember. e.g. *Kens father* (Who owns the father? *Ken*. Put the apostrophe after *Ken*. That, is write *Ken's father*.

Remember: You don't need an apostrophe simply to make a plural noun, e.g. *The hikers arrived at camp*. NOT *The hikers' arrived at camp* OR *The hiker's arrived at camp*.

Put the apostrophe in the right place in these examples.

1
- **a** no mans land
- **b** his fathers adventures
- **c** the (two) dogs harnesses
- **d** the two young explorers route
- **e** the tents opening
- **f** the womens expedition
- **g** the suns glare
- **h** the mans loneliness

2 Tick the sentences that are punctuated correctly.
- **a** The icy rain bit into the lone climber's eyes. ______
- **b** The boys father was the last to reach the summit. ______
- **c** The commandos trained for hours. ______
- **d** The cliff's edge lay centimetres' from them. ______
- **e** The cyclist's muscles ached for hours afterwards. ______

Select a word

Choose words from the vocabulary list that mean the same as these words.

1 icy coldness ______________________

2 lacking ______________________

3 with one voice ______________________

4 stupidity ______________________

5 nothingness ______________________

6 in a very determined way ______________________

7 never stopping or lessening ______________________

8 thought deeply ______________________

Grammar

Non-finite *-ing* clauses

- Look at the underlined parts of these sentences:
  Stumbling, he made his way forward.
  He trudged onwards, his vision blurring from the glare of the sun.
- The underlined parts are a type of **dependent clause.** (That is, they add a unit of meaning to the main clause.)
- These examples use *~ing* forms of the verb (the present participle) but *~ed* or other 'past participle' forms can be used as well, e.g. *Whipped by the wind, they retreated. Beaten at the last minute, they cried in despair.*

- Because they are not full (or 'finite') verbs, we call these kinds of clauses **non-finite clauses**.
- This type of dependent clause is useful when we want to talk about two actions that are going on at about the same time.
- You need to take care that the dependent clause relates clearly and sensibly to a noun in the main clause, e.g.
  Climbing out of the ditch, the dogs waited patiently. (This sounds as if the dogs were climbing out of the ditch and also waiting patiently.)

  One way to correct it is:
  Climbing out of the ditch, he saw his dogs waiting patiently.

Note: In some books you may find these kinds of clauses called **participial phrases**.

1 In these sentences, underline the dependent clauses using ~*ing* verbs.

e.g. *Whistling, he rode away.*

a He fell, crying out with pain.

b The ice closed in, trapping him without mercy.

c The sun beat down steadily, burning into his reddened flesh.

d Keeping himself quite still, he listened for other human sounds.

e The other expedition members, believing he had been killed, finally abandoned the camp site.

2 Correct these sentences so that they make sense.

a Running along, a rock fell on his head.

b Crawling into the base camp, the lights were shining.

c Believing his time had come, the polar bear approached.

____

____

____

Word study

There are many powerful adjectives we can use to describe people or things. What adjectives can we use to describe the people and things below? Use a thesaurus to help you.

1 the cold ______________________________

2 the heat ______________________________

3 the night ______________________________

4 the desert ______________________________

5 the city ______________________________

Evaluating other people's writing

Look at the opening to the student's story below. It is an effective opening—similar in some ways to 'The journey' and different in others. Identify the similarities and differences. Think about, for example:

- the opening words
- the subject of the story
- the setting for the story (time and place)
- the particular aspect of the subject the writer focuses on (thoughts, appearance, actions)
- the mood the writer creates (serious, mysterious, humorous, dramatic)
- the language used to create an image
- the use of action verbs to describe what the subject does

Calling home

Light poured from a sole streetlight and pounded down upon Frank's balding head. His eyes flicked down the empty shop fronts ... nothing ... no-one ... empty ... silent. Not even the sounds of distant cars speeding by.

Completely natural for 3 am. This was perfect. It was his kind of time. This felt right.

Frank was dirty. His ancient brown boots were wet and muddy, his black jeans decrepit and torn. The long brown coat slung over his shoulders was scruffed and faded from long, hard years of wear. His pockets were ripped and filled with holes. And a piece of old gum adorned a sleeve.

But it didn't matter. No-one would ever look twice at him. Frank was no pretty picture. His was an unshaven face. His nose and cheeks drooped like wilted roses. Partly because that was the way he was, and partly because he'd been drinking hard liquor—and plenty of it.

Frank's brain twitched as his eyes moved past the barred door of the liquormart.

Nick Henderson

____

____

____

Quick think

Fill in the blanks with words you could use instead of 'walk'.

1	move like a snake	_ l _ th _ _
2	walk without lifting your feet off the ground, as if wearing slippers	sh _ _ _ le
3	walk with slow steps as if your feet are heavy	p _ o _
4	walk as if you are going to fall or as if you have been hurt badly	s _ a _ _ er
5	walk in a slow relaxed manner	_ _ r _ ll
6	walk unevenly and slowly, as if one leg is hurt	l _ _ p

Proofreading

Punctuate the next two paragraphs of 'Calling home' (above) with full stops and commas.

Frank slithered backwards and collapsed on the kerb it felt gritty and hard a cold wind picked up and blew past a copy of yesterday's news then all was quiet once again picking himself up unsteadily Frank scratched his brow then looked up and saw it was a cloudy starless sky.

In the distance a payphone emitted a soulless fluorescent light Frank's weary feet shuffled and slowly began to drag his battered old body towards it.

Writing paragraphs and whole texts

1 Here are the remaining paragraphs of 'Calling home'. However, the verbs are missing. Complete the story using the verbs below.

clanged, pushing, fell, meshed, stumbled, dangled, fumbled, clinging

His two old hands **a** ________________ inside his coat pockets for change. His eyes seemed reluctant to open to the obscene blinding of the fluorescent tube. Three coins **b** ________________ into the abyss of the phone slot. It was the last of Frank's resources. With one hand **c** ________________ onto the receiver, he **d** ________________ his scroungy fingers against the buttons, **e** ________________ a pattern familiar to him. He could hear the cold electronic noise of dialling, and then the awkward ring. Four times it rang before anyone picked it up.

'Jane, hi ... it's papa ... Jane?'

Silence. Click. Beep, beep, beep. A coin **f** ________________ as it fell down the refund chute.

Frank **g** ________________ backwards. The receiver **h** ________________ lifelessly. It began to rain.

2 Here is the first paragraph from a story by Amber Hopkins called 'It's all about luck'.

Brandon sat staring at the cards in his hand. He glanced up around the table, wishing the other guys would show some emotion. Just a look of despair to let him know they had bust, or of smugness to let him know they had twenty-one. But these guys were professionals. They had the 'poker-face' look perfected. He wouldn't get any help from them.

Put these remaining paragraphs from the story into the order that tells the story.

a Brandon stared down now at the ring and the life savings on the table. I've got to win this time, he thought desperately. All I need is a four. A four or under. Even an ace, worth one, would be okay. He put his cards down slowly. Please, please God, let it be a four. If you grant me one favour in this life, let this be it. If it's a four, I get twenty-one and win. If it's higher, I'll bust, and lose everything.

b Brandon looked around nervously. You could cut the tension with a knife, as they say. He felt the sweat trickle down his neck. The other guys were getting impatient. What to do? He had a lot staked on this game. He couldn't lose. He couldn't ...

c The other men looked at him. Even they looked nervous. 'Well?' the dealer said. 'Do you want another card or not?'

d *It was a five.*

e He thought back to a few hours ago. He and Maggie had just had another argument about why he couldn't invest their life savings in Blackjack. He had had her engagement ring in his pocket as they argued. When she had asked a little later where her ring was, he had spun her a story about taking it to the jeweller to get it widened, in response to her complaints about it being too tight. She had kissed him and asked if he had enough money to cover it. He assured her he had enough, and felt anxiously for the life savings he had hidden in his sock.

f 'Yes' Brandon croaked. The dealer flicked him a card face down. He squinted his eyes shut and picked up the card. Please, a four, a four, he thought. He slowly opened his eyes and looked at the card in his hand.

g Brandon looked down again at the two cards in his hand. A ten and a seven. The worst cards he could imagine. You couldn't win on it, but ask for another card and you'd surely go bust. And he couldn't afford to do that.

3 Write a short story on the theme of 'The journey'. Your subject could be a real, physical journey of some sort, or a mental or emotional journey as in 'Calling home' or 'It's all about luck', or it could be both, as with 'The journey'.

Follow these steps:

- Begin the story in the way that the writer of the three stories in this chapter did, immediately orienting your reader to the subject and setting the scene. Develop the image of the subject for the reader with details about his or her thoughts, appearance, movements and so on.
- Introduce some complication—an event that gives the story interest and makes it more than just a recount of a series of events. In other words, <u>something has to happen</u>.
- Resolve your story either wholly or partly. It is sometimes more interesting <u>not</u> to resolve all the events and problems, but to leave the reader with some questions unanswered.

Use the space below for your notes and planning.

News article

STRUCTURE

overall structure reflects dual text purpose—to inform and interest the reader

headline that gives topic and attracts reader

headline often plays with words in some way

first paragraph gives important information and attracts reader's interest

emphasis on reporting of events

events not always reported in order in which they occurred in the 'real world'

paragraphs often quite short—even one sentence

often no clear topic sentences in paragraphs

Try to buy before you steal

A would-be thief was left with nothing more than an empty feeling yesterday when a counter server at McDonald's told him he couldn't rob the restaurant without buying something.

Eager to oblige, the intruder searched his pockets but could find only 30 cents. The counter assistant hadn't ever experienced such a confrontation, so he went looking for the manager.

But the frustrated intruder apparently changed his mind and fled empty-handed.

He had run into the Circular Quay store shortly before 10 am, produced a knife and demanded money, police said.

He was described as a tall, dark-haired Caucasian in his late 30s, wearing a baseball cap, a shiny sports jacket, dark jeans and a green T-shirt.

Sydney Morning Herald

Botanic gardens ritual: it's a blooming mystery

by Ellen Connelly

It is a daily ritual, a gentle crusade by a phantom benefactor. Every day for the past 548 days, a single fresh flower has been placed in the hands of the shy young girl in the *I Wish* sculpture in the Royal Botanic Gardens.

'It's quite intriguing and really is a total mystery,' the director of the gardens, Mr Frank Howarth, said yesterday. 'Nobody has seen them putting the flower there.'

Parallels had been drawn with the eccentric Arthur Stace, who for 40 years wrote his copperplate 'Eternity' message across Sydney.

'The most common analogy, though, that I've heard is of the woman who delivered roses to the grave of Rudolph Valentino every day for years and years,' Mr Howarth said.

Mr Howarth said the flower ritual began 18 months ago when the statue was moved closer to the path to accommodate a new plant.

The flowers vary, depending on the season. Yesterday it was a camellia, last week azaleas, and sometimes lilies. There are no plans to discover who is placing the flowers. 'That would destroy the mystery. It's better not to know.'

Sydney Morning Herald

LANGUAGE FEATURES

lot of information in a sentence

action verbs, e.g. 'fled'

pronouns to link ideas through text, e.g. 'he'

saying verbs, e.g. 'said', 'described'

usually past tense because it is about what has already happened

direct speech within quotation marks

indirect speech

Comprehension

The structure of newspaper articles helps us to get the main idea about the reported events immediately—generally in the headline and in the first paragraph. This structure is a response to the way people read newspapers (whether in print or online)—they sometimes read the whole article, but at other times they only skim for the essentials of the story. Sometimes they may be looking for one detail only.

1 What is 'Try to buy before you steal' about? Underline the correct answer.

a a major robbery **b** a minor robbery **c** an attempted robbery

Where did you find the information? ______________________________

2 What is 'Botanic gardens ritual: it's a blooming mystery' about? Underline the correct answer.

a a new statue in the Royal Botanic Gardens

b a mystery about a statue in the Royal Botanic Gardens

c a new director for the Royal Botanic Gardens

Where did you find the information? ______________________________

3 Look back at the first report and answer true or false.

a The thief bought an ice-cream. ____________________

b The counter server refused to give the thief money. ____________________

c The counter server did not leave the counter. ____________________

d The police found the thief at Circular Quay. ____________________

4 Look back at the second report and answer true or false.

a The statue in the garden is of a young girl. ____________________

b A young girl places a flower in the statue's hands every day. ____________________

c The director wants to know who is putting the flower in the statue's hands. ____________________

d The statue was moved 18 months ago. ____________________

5 What do the words in italics refer to in these sentences?

a ... so *he* went looking for the manager. ____________________

b *He* had run into the Circular Quay store ... ____________________

c Nobody has seen *them* putting the flower there. ____________________

d Yesterday *it* was a camellia, last week azaleas, and sometimes lilies. ____________________

Writing skills

News writers do not always report information in the order that it happened in the real world because this may not be the most interesting way; they place the most important and/or most interesting information first and then give other details. This makes the **structure of a news report** quite different from that of other factual reports.

1 Place the events below from 'Try to buy...' in the order that they actually occurred.

a Counter assistant asks McDonald's manager for help. ______

b Man leaves restaurant. ______

c Counter assistant tells thief that he can't steal if he has not bought anything. ______

d Man searches his pockets for money. ______

e Man pulls a knife and demands money in McDonald's restaurant. ______

Which of these was the first event reported in the article? ______

2 Count the number of sentences in each paragraph of the two stories. Why do you think writers often use very short paragraphs? The information above may help you.

______

______

3 'Botanic gardens ritual' uses the actual words that a person in the story spoke, but 'Try to buy ...' does not. Imagine you were writing 'Try to buy ...'. Whose words would be good to use? Write down an example of what he or she might say. Remember to use quotation marks ('...').

______

______

4 'Try to buy ...' has a humorous element. Underline the words in the article which show that the writer thinks the story is funny.

Vocabulary

would-be	**oblige**	**intruder**	**experiences**	**confrontation**
frustrated	**apparently**	**fled**	**Caucasian**	**mystery**
crusade	**phantom**	**benefactor**	**sculpture**	**intriguing**
parallels	**eccentric**	**copperplate**	**analogy**	**accommodate**

One way to remember a tricky part of a word is to think of an image that helps you to remember it. For example, thinking of the two bars used for the parallel bars gymnastics event may help you remember that there is a double 'l' in the word *parallel*—the two bars are like the two 'l's. Can you think of a way to remember the double letters in *accommodate*, *apparently* and *eccentric*?

Learn all the words in the vocabulary list now using the Look, Cover, Write, Check method.

Now cover up the word list and test your memory to make corrections where needed in these sentences. (Write in the space.)

1 He is very expirienced in wood and brass sculpture. ______

2 Kara's tastes in painting and sculpture are rather ecentric. ______

3 Apparently the identity of the thief is still a mystiry. ______

4 How intriguing that no-one noticed the sculpture was missing! ______

5 There is space to accomodate ten new pieces of sculpture. ______

Focus on punctuation

Quotation marks

- We use quotation marks or inverted commas ('…') whenever we write the exact words that someone has said. You may use single or double quotation marks.
- If the quotation comes before *he said/asked*, we use a comma or question mark at its end before closing the quotation marks.
- If the quotation comes after *he said/asked*, we put a full stop, or question mark, at its end before closing the quotation marks.

e.g. *'It's quite intriguing and really is a total mystery,' the director of the gardens, Mr Frank Howarth, said yesterday. 'Nobody has seen them putting the flower there.'*

Important: You don't need to use inverted commas when you are **reporting** what someone said (reported or indirect speech). Compare the above (direct speech) with the following (indirect speech): *Mr Howarth said that it was quite intriguing and really was a total mystery.*

1 Put quotation marks and other punctuation where needed in these extracts from news stories.

- **a** We are asking everyone to take care in the area the spokesman said.
- **b** Most people don't realise how demanding writing is said the famous author. They think you sit down and the words just flow out.
- **c** We hold grave fears for his safety said the sergeant in charge. The situation is very grim.
- **d** I've been through hell the young surfer said after being chased by a 2-metre shark.
- **e** The zoo worker said I was simply doing my daily job, feeding the bears when she suddenly turned on me.
- **f** His memory is not good and we are worried that he might have gone off somewhere the old man's daughter said tearfully.

2 Which of the following is punctuated correctly?

- **a** 'Can someone please help me,' the sales assistant cried out.
- **b** 'Can someone please help me?' the sales assistant cried out.
- **c** Can someone please help me? the sales assistant cried out.
- **d** 'Can someone please help me' the sales assistant cried out.

Select a word

Choose words from the vocabulary list that have the same meanings as these words.

1 difficult or hostile meeting ____________________

2 likeness, similarity ____________________

3 matches, is similar to ____________________

4 a person who supports someone or something ____________________

5 someone who does very unusual things ____________________

6 do what is asked/expected ____________________

7 find space for ____________________

8 white, European ____________________

Grammar

Verbs—past tense forms

- When we talk about events that happened in the past we choose between three main forms:
  - past, e.g. *he ran, he was running*
  - present perfect, e.g. *he has run, he has been running*
  - past perfect, e.g. *he had run, he had been running*
- You do not need to remember the names of these tense forms, but it is important to understand their different functions and to choose the right one when you write.
- One way to do this is to take notice of the tenses other writers use.

- Look at the two news articles.

  'Try to buy ...' mostly uses the **past** because the events described are completed, e.g.
  But the frustrated intruder apparently changed his mind and fled empty-handed.

  It also uses the **past perfect** to talk about an event that happened before these events, e.g.
  He had run into the Circular Quay store shortly before 10 am ...

  'Botanic gardens ritual...' uses the **present perfect** in some parts because it is about events that are still happening, e.g.
  Nobody has seen them putting the flower there.

1 Look back at the news articles and underline all the verbs. Think about why the particular tense form has been chosen.

2 Complete these sentences with the correct tense forms of the verb in brackets.

a Police last night ______________________ (search) rugged bushland for a teenage boy who ______________________ (go missing) after a furious row with his parents.

b The man who discovered the hidden money, ______________________ (bushwalk) with friends.

c The fighting ______________________ (go on) for two weeks now.

d A sick young Melbourne girl ______________________ (discover) that she is about to receive one million dollars from a mystery benefactor.

e A neighbour last ______________________ (see) him in the front garden on Friday, but before that she ______________________ (see) him many times walking around the area, and he ______________________ (seem) fine.

Word study

Headline writers must attract the readers' attention and tell them what the story is about in a very small space. They do this by:

- choosing brief, dramatic words, e.g. *Blast kills 20* (an explosion kills 20 people)
- leaving out certain words, e.g. *30 workers sacked* (30 workers have been sacked)
- using a string of nouns, e.g. *Police death mystery* (there is a mystery about the death of a policeman)

Match these headline words with their meanings.

CLASH	DEAL	AXE	BLAZE
BAN	SWOOP	BOOST	CUT
DRIVE	HIT	KEY	PLEA

a agreement
b request for help
c very important, critical
d reduction (to pay, hours, services etc.)
e negatively affected
f campaign, effort
g conflict, dispute
h stop, take away
i fire
j prohibition, forbidden
k help, encouragement
l sudden attack or raid

Evaluating other people's writing

Look at this first draft of a newspaper article. Mark at least five things in the article that could be improved, e.g.

- the headline
- the order of the information
- paragraphing
- tense forms
- the amount of information given about the events
- the language used to give the information
- use of people's own words to talk about events

Young boy bitten

A young boy called Tim Roberts was playing in the yard with friends when a funnel-web spider bit him. He was at his local playground at the time of the bite. He cries out in pain and his friends go over to get his mother from her home. By this time Tim is unconscious. The spider was under Tim's singlet so it could have been there for a long time. Tim is now in the local hospital in the intensive care unit. He had been taken to the hospital last night and given the anti-venene for funnel-webs. His parents are only now relaxing because Tim seems to be doing OK.

Quick think

Headlines often have a double meaning. Sometimes a headline may include a reference to a well-known saying. Sometimes it may combine two aspects of the story in the article.

For example, in the headline 'Botanic gardens ritual: it's a blooming mystery', the word *blooming* has two meanings:

- growing healthily, blossoming (as with flowers)
- great (similar meaning to the slang word 'bloody')

Match the headlines (1–4) to the story summaries (a–d), thinking about the double meaning of the words.

1 A LOAD OF RUBBISH!	**a** story about a pub that had to refund customers' money after discovering contaminated beer
2 FOOD FOR THOUGHT	**b** report on the challenges of operating a café or restaurant
3 WHAT A STINK!	**c** residents taking a chicken shop to court about the smell of the fumes from its chimney
4 DRINKS ON US	**d** company charged with dumping chemical waste after previously denying it

Proofreading

Which words are spelt incorrectly? Correct any mistakes you find and then check them against the chapter vocabulary list.

would-be	oblige	introoder	experences	confrentation
frusterated	aparently	fled	Caucasian	mistry
crusade	fantom	benfactor	sculpture	intreging
paralels	ecentric	copperplate	analogy	accomodate

Writing paragraphs and whole texts

1 Complete these sentences with the correct past tense form of the verb in brackets.

A tourist **a** _______________ (survive) a 16-kilometre swim through crocodile and shark-infested waters after being thrown overboard from a yacht off Cairns. Karla French, 30, from Belgium, **b** _______________ (say) she was thrown from the yacht which **c** _______________ (head) for Lizard Island. She **d** _______________ (manage) to reach a remote island where she was stranded for two days and two nights. With temperatures soaring, Ms French **e** _______________ (drink) salt water to quench her thirst. She then **f** _______________ (decide) to swim for the coast, 16 kilometres away. Five hours after she **g** _______________ (set off), she was circled by what she **h** _______________ (describe) as a huge shark. She **i** _______________ (make) it to Cooktown at 8 pm Friday night. In an extraordinary stroke of luck, she was spotted on the beach by a worker on a nearby sandmine. The man **j** _______________ (drive) along the beach at the time. Ms French **k** _______________ (thank) her rescuer and the police but did not want to press charges against the person who **l** _______________ (throw) her overboard. She **m** _______________ (recover) last night in Cooktown hospital.

2 Look back at the text in 1 above. Read it through and put a stroke (/) wherever you think a new paragraph is needed. Remember: newspaper paragraphs are usually quite short and often contain only one sentence.

3 Cut out some short newspaper articles from your local or metropolitan newspaper. Read the articles, taking particular notice of:

- the words used in the headline
- the way the first paragraph sums up the important ideas
- the length of the paragraphs
- use of direct and indirect speech to report what people said
- the tense forms used to tell the story
- the order in which the events are reported

4 Write an imaginary newspaper article on a topic or event of interest, using the articles in this chapter and your own collection as models. (You could rewrite the news article in 'Evaluating other people's writing', if you cannot think of a topic.)

Use the space below and on the next page to jot down ideas or to make plans for what you will include and in what order you will report the events. (Tip: keep it simple. Don't try to tell a complicated tale. Perhaps choose a theft or other crime, a lost-and-found story about a missing person, a good news event, or a person saved from danger.)

CHAPTER 9

Short opinion texts: blogposts and letters to the editor

STRUCTURE

overall structure reflects text purpose: to express opinion and persuade the reader

introduction identifies the topic (usually by reference to earlier post/ letter or article) and opinion

mixture of fact and opinion

generally quite short and to the point

short, concise sentences

direct appeal to the editor/ reader

often only one paragraph

if more than one, additional paragraphs give evidence to support opinion

paragraph length varies

conclusion sums up or repeats opinion; may contain a question, request, suggestion or warning

From Stanway High e-newsletter

The World Vision 40 Hour Famine will be held over the weekend of 25–27 August. Our school has been involved in this wonderful cause for 20 years now.

Blogposts

Text 1

26 June 2023

Hey! The 40 Hour Famine is upon us. There are no downsides to standing up for this brilliant cause. Except of course the personal discomfort, hunger and pain you might feel as the hours go on! BUT, think of this. You'll be helping the 45 million children in the world who are on the brink of hunger this very minute. They're feeling exactly the same way right now and for much longer than a weekend. So no excuses guys. Last year the Year 9 total was the best in the school. So let's do that again this year but smash the 20-year record as well!

40 Hour Famine Year 9 Committee

Text 2

27 June 2023

Who could disagree with Year 9 (26 June)? None of us have any excuse NOT to join in the 40 Hour challenge. And if competing with each other helps raise more money, that's awesome. But we don't need to get carried away with who's the best. Last year there was some ugly behaviour over class tallies. Anything we can do will help vulnerable children in need. And remember: it doesn't have to involve fasting.

School Organising Committee

From the Stanway Gazette 28 and 29 August 2023

AUSSIE FILM ICONS TAKE UP THE CHALLENGE

CELEBRITIES AGAIN SHOW 40 HOUR GENEROSITY

Stars come out for 40 hour famine

Letters to the editor 5 and 10 September 2023

Text 3

More balanced reporting

I'm writing in regard to your recent headlines (28 and 29 August, 2023) about the contributions of celebrities to this Year's 40 Hour Famine success. Not one but two issues praised their attendance and contribution.

While I too am appreciative of well-known people taking part and understand the power they have to encourage others to do likewise, I believe the media focus on them is too great. There should be far more attention paid to the thousands who take part without any acknowledgement at all.

In particular, the efforts of the thousands of school students who participate should be given more coverage. Instead these efforts, in your newspaper at least, are given only a few lines. So how about doing better next year?

Miri Lambert

Text 4

School achievements for World Vision

Re 'More balanced reporting' (5 September 2023) we agree completely, though at the same time we acknowledge the generosity of the celebrities who take part.

Many schools across Australia organise their own events: endurance runs, 'Stay outdoors' challenges, community service, and so on. How great it would have been if your newspaper had given at least some space to these efforts?

Our school raised $20 000 with a Sports Olympiad this year. How about an article on that?

Arif Aziz / Cal Costanza

LANGUAGE FEATURES

blogposts and letters begin with a reference to a previous post, letter or article (but some may start a conversation about a topic)

persuasive language and content, e.g. 'no downsides', 'so no excuses'

modal forms to show strength of opinion, e.g. 'might', 'should', 'can'

personal language can be included particularly in a blogpost, e.g. 'we', 'you', 'let's'

blogposts typically feature less formal language than letters to the editor, e.g. rhetorical questions, capitals or other punctuation to emphasise points

subjective language to express your own view; should not be too emotional

respect for other writers and readers in content and language

Comprehension

Both the blogposts and letters to the editor on page 66 have the purpose of persuading the reader to agree with a point of view on a current issue. Letters to the editor almost always have this purpose but blogposts may have other purposes, such as recounting events or entertaining the reader.

Blogposts and letters to the editor are often a response to an earlier piece of writing: an article or an earlier blogpost or letter, for example. However, it should be easy to understand the general topic without having read the earlier item. They should give details about when and where this item appeared so the reader can search for it if they want to.

1 Which blogpost/letter (Text 1, 2, 3 or 4) is mainly about the

a inappropriate focus on celebrity involvement in the 40 Hour Famine? ______

b reason for taking part in the 40 Hour Famine fundraising? ______

c appropriate way to go about fundraising for the 40 Hour Famine? ______

d different ways that schools get involved in the 40 Hour Famine? ______

2 What do you believe is the main purpose of the two letters to the editor?

a to make the editor and the public think about what is worth reporting

b to get more young people to do the 40-hour famine

c to get more recognition of young people's contributions

d to criticise the participation of celebrities

3 How does the writer of the first blogpost (Text 1) compare the students doing the 40 Hour Famine to children living in hunger?

____

4 Which best expresses the view of the writers of the second blogpost (Text 2) about fundraising competition between classes?

a They believe competition is the best way to raise funds.

b They totally disapprove of any competition between classes.

c They believe students should only focus on one reason for fundraising.

d They believe competition can help raise funds but caution against too much focus on this.

5 One blogpost and one letter approve of a strategy to increase funds raised while at the same time express criticism of too much focus on this strategy. What are the two methods and which texts refer to them?

Strategy	**Text**
______________________	______
______________________	______

Writing skills

Writers of persuasive texts such as blogposts and letters to the editor use many **persuasive language devices** to express their view and to persuade readers to agree with them.

1 For each text, which of the following writing devices are used by the writer?

	Text 1	Text 2	Text 3	Text 4
Direct appeal to the reader	______	______	______	______
Direct appeal to the editor	______	______	______	______
Factual evidence	______	______	______	______
Logical argument	______	______	______	______
Emotional language	______	______	______	______
Comparison/Contrast	______	______	______	______
Personal experience	______	______	______	______

2 In blogposts you can be more subjective, even emotional, and include more personal information. However, you still need to write in a way that shows you have thought properly about the topic; otherwise readers will pay little attention to your argument.

a Look at the two blogposts. Underline or write below any examples of emotional or personal language used.

____

b Which blogpost was more informal? ________

3 Look at the letters to the editor. Underline the words used to express more appropriately (more formally, less emotionally and personally) the ideas below.

a Stop giving so much attention to these rich and famous people.

b I get it that famous people bring in the money.

c You didn't mention all the awesome stuff done by schools for this event.

Vocabulary

except	**exactly**	**committee**	**competing**	**behaviour**
contributions	**celebrities**	**success**	**issues**	**praise**
encourage	**acknowledgement**	**particular**	**coverage**	**vulnerable**
balance	**completely**	**generosity**	**endurance**	**challenges**

1 Break the words up into syllables (sound chunks) and then learn them using the Look, Cover, Write, Check method. Make sure you have at least one letter per syllable in each word. This makes you think closely about how the word is constructed and makes it less likely you will make an error with longer words.

2 Now cover up the word list and test your memory to make corrections where needed in these sentences. (Write in the space.)

a The principal invited two local celebreties to open the sports challange. ________________

b There was almost no acknowlegement of the contribtions of students. ________________

c The principal encourraged everyone to particpate this year. ________________

d The genrosity of the two actors was outstanding. ________________

e Prase was heaped on the endurence runners who raised $2000. ________________

f The newspaper gave covrage to the event in both morning and evening ishues. ________________

Focus on punctuation

Capital letters

- We use **capital letters** for **proper names** of specific people (Uncle John), places (Niagara Falls), institutions (Commonwealth Bank), official positions (General Manager), languages (English), races (Indian), countries (New Zealand) and events (Fashion Week).
- We also use capital letters for the **first, last and every important word in titles** of books, films, reports and so on (although writers vary considerably in how they do this).
- We usually don't use capital letters in newspaper article headlines except for first words and names of people etc. (Of course, many newspaper headlines are completely in capital letters.)

1 Look back at the blogposts and letters to the editor and underline all the words and groups of words that are capitalised. In each case, think about why they are capitalised.

2 Put capitals where required in these sentences. (Note: You would also need to use inverted commas or italics for titles or books, films, magazines etc.)

a The article first appeared in the shepparton news but I heard about it on the sunrise show.

b The cast from neighbours in 1994 committed to the whole 40 hour challenge.

c the tour went to uluru and alice springs as well as other less known parts of the northern territory.

d In 1997 the abc television show heartbreak high staged a school sleepover for its characters to draw attention to the 40 hour famine.

e The students of summerdale high raised $10 000 with their famine sleepover at summerdale stadium.

f I read to kill a mockingbird in Year 9 but haven't read the sequel go set a watchman.

Select a word

Choose words from the vocabulary list that mean the same as these words.

1 stating that you are aware of something ____________________

2 the amount of space or attention given to a news event ____________________

3 in need of special care or protection ____________________

4 the ability to keep going when faced with difficulties ____________________

5 kindness and willingness to give money or time ____________________

6 something that is difficult to do ____________________

7 even-handed treatment ____________________

8 magazine or newspaper editions ____________________

Grammar

Dependent clauses

- Remember: A **sentence** is a group of words that expresses a complete thought and that can stand alone. A sentence has a subject (a **noun** or **noun group**) and a verb (or **verb group**).
- Sentences may have
  - only one clause (a **simple sentence**)
  - two or more equal main clauses (a **compound sentence**), or
  - one main 'stand-alone' clause and one or more dependent clauses (a **complex sentence**).
- **Dependent clauses** mostly begin with **conjunctions** such as *because*, *when*, *if*, *after*, *whereas*, or words like *who*, *whose*, *whom*, *which* or *that* (**relative pronouns**). However, as shown in Chapter 7, they sometimes begin with an *-ing* or *-ed* form of the verb (non-finite clauses).

- Dependent clauses are <u>not</u> sentences. These are <u>not</u> sentences:
  Participating for the tenth year in a row.
  Compared with other year groups.
  Which has become a rite of passage for many young Australians and New Zealanders.
- If we link these with 'stand-alone' clauses, they <u>do</u> form sentences.
  Participating for the tenth year in a row, Medlow North are expecting their best performance yet.
  Year 9 had more varied options to choose from compared with other year groups.
  The 40 Hour Famine, which has become a rite of passage for many young Australians and New Zealanders, takes place on the last weekend of next month.

1 Match these main clauses with these dependent clauses in a way that makes sense.

Main clause	Dependent clause
1 I think you give too much attention to models and actresses.	**a** whereas the people in the other article were wasting time and money.
2 I wrote to you	**b** when we read the article.
3 My parents and I were deeply offended	**c** so that you would understand young people.
4 These young people were doing good	**d** if you really wanted to.
5 You could put this article on the front page	**e** though I know you think your readers want this.

2 Now underline the dependent clauses in these sentences. Note: the dependent clause is sometimes in the middle of a sentence, e.g. *<u>The girl who won</u> accepted her prize.*

a The class voted for the charity that they wished to support for the year.
b They awarded a prize to the boys whose project raised the most money.
c Everyone attended the auction which was expected to raise $10 000.
d The students who did the walkathon raised $3000 for the local charity.
e The event that we were all looking forward to so much was cancelled at the last minute.

3 Which of these are sentences and which are only dependent clauses? Write S for Sentence and DC for Dependent Clause.

a If teenagers had something to do. ____________
b We had a wonderful time at the event although we were hungry and cold. ____________
c After the success of last year's event. ____________
d Because young people want to contribute to society. ____________
e When young people work together, they can achieve great things. ____________
f Which disappointed us all. ____________
g The students who finished the walk cheered us on. ____________
h Which now cannot be held because of bad weather. ____________

Word study

You should try to avoid very emotional language in letters to the editor because it can offend. It can also make you look like an unreasonable, biased individual. However, sometimes emotional language is appropriate, especially if you are writing about an extreme and serious situation.

Use your dictionary to rate these words from most emotional (1) to least emotional (3). (Note that the meanings of the words in each group are not identical.)

1 sickening ( ), troubling ( ), distressing ( )

2 insulted ( ), offended ( ), unsettled ( )

3 regretful ( ), embarrassed ( ), mortified ( )

4 unwise ( ), ridiculous ( ), foolish ( )

Evaluating other people's writing

What is wrong with the letter to the editor opposite? Mark at least five things in the letter that could be improved, e.g.

- clarity of purpose
- organisation and clarity of ideas
- development of ideas
- vocabulary and grammar
- punctuation

I was recently at city station and had a sickening experience. I could hear a man yelling and screaming at a customer in the most abusive way. I wondered what could be the matter so I walked up the station to have a look. I gradually understood that the problem was that the customer did not have a ticket. Attempting to explain this to the young guard. I could not believe my eyes really and think that the railways people should do more about training their staff to handle problems better. Especially after reading last week in your paper about abuse of old people getting worse in some places. You see the customer was about 75 and had a walking stick and I guess the guard thought he was fair game.

Quick think

These words are useful to describe the way you feel about a situation:

outraged, appalled, disgusted, ashamed, distressed, concerned, unsettled, anxious, troubled, saddened, shocked, disturbed, encouraged, delighted.

Find as many of the words as you can in the wordsearch below.

D	A	P	P	X	T	S	R	C	O	N	C	E	R	N	E	D	D	D
E	A	X	O	R	P	R	A	S	E	U	O	G	E	F	S	R	E	I
L	P	S	A	D	D	E	N	E	D	E	T	G	E	F	H	O	X	S
I	P	O	H	M	M	O	P	A	B	C	O	R	F	O	O	G	I	T
G	A	O	Z	A	N	X	I	O	U	S	Z	M	A	N	C	N	A	U
H	L	N	Y	O	M	F	E	E	M	D	M	O	Z	G	K	A	H	R
T	L	F	X	R	G	E	E	U	N	S	E	T	T	L	E	D	R	B
E	E	G	R	Z	O	P	D	I	S	G	U	S	T	E	D	D	O	E
D	D	I	S	T	R	E	S	S	E	D	T	R	O	U	B	L	E	D
X	E	N	C	O	U	R	A	G	E	D	O	O	C	K	D	E	L	L

Proofreading

Put full stops, commas and question marks in this letter to the editor.

> I was horrified recently to hear that a young woman convicted of tripping up an old man and stealing his money was given a two year good behaviour bond the old man was hospitalised for two months from injuries he received where is the justice in our society why aren't people put in jail for violent crimes like this if they are not then they will think that these are not serious crimes and commit them again very soon I believe it is time to review our sentencing practices.

Writing paragraphs and whole texts

1 Imagine you want to write a follow-up blogpost to those written by the 40 Hour Year 9 Committee and the School Organising Committee on page 66. You agree in some way with both posts. Which of these beginnings would be best? Think about the clarity of the link to the previous posts and how well your introduction points to what might come next.

- **a** Last year Year 8 came last in the tally and everyone made fun of us.
- **b** Both the Year 9 Committee (26/6) and the School Committee (27/6) have good ideas.
- **c** I think both the Year 9 Committee (26/6) and the School Committee (27/6) want to help as many children as possible and both see a role for competition. However, ...
- **d** Everyone protests about too much competition but come on guys secretly we all love it.
- **e** The Year 9 Committee (26/6) and the School Committee (27/6) talk about the 40 Hour Famine.

2 Put the paragraphs from this letter to the editor into an order that makes sense.

- **a** What I cannot understand is why there was not more attention given to this production in your newspaper. The school, of course, had an advertisement in the entertainment pages and advertised widely in the community.
- **b** I don't really know where to begin in describing the talent and enthusiasm that I witnessed. It is impossible to single out one performer or one aspect of the production. Let me say, however, that I have seen this musical produced professionally in the city and that I enjoyed this one even more.
- **c** So, well done, kids! And next time, how about some free publicity for our school performances?
- **d** However, I don't think it is too much to ask for the local newspaper to give some free publicity to such ventures. This would enable the maximum number of people to get to see it. I am sure some people missed it because they did not know it was on.
- **e** Recently I had the privilege of being in the audience of the local school production of *West Side Story*. I want to let readers know that, if they did not see it, they missed a truly impressive piece of musical theatre, and to say congratulations to the entire cast and crew.

____

3 Write a blogpost in response to the two on page 66. Imagine you are at the school in Year 9 and want to support the view in one or both posts. Use the beginning sentences in 1 above in any way you wish. You could also use ideas from the letters to the editor about newspaper coverage of celebrities if you wish. Be sure to include your opinions about the cause and about the use of competition between years. While you can show some emotion, don't go too far—and remember to respect other writers and your readers.

____

____

4 Look in a recent newspaper (metropolitan or local) and find an article (or two) that makes you think. Write a letter to the editor on your own paper in response to the article. Use the space below for notes and drafting. Or imagine you are following up the ideas in the two letters on page 66, supporting or opposing the views given. You may have your own experiences to add.

CHAPTER 10

Biography

STRUCTURE

overall structure reflects text purpose—to give information about a person's life

introduction, which gives name of person and why he/she was famous

focus on recounting facts about person's life

paragraphs about different stages or aspects of person's life—generally in chronological sequence

careful selection of detail about person's life

specific information about time and place

may or may not be conclusion, but last paragraph often includes some comment on person's life or contribution

Martin Luther King

Martin Luther King was the leader of the Civil Rights Movement against racism in the United States of America during the 1950s and 1960s. Tragically, at the age of 39 he was shot dead.

King was born in 1929 in Atlanta, Georgia, in the deep south of the USA, where the segregation of black people and white people was a way of life. In most southern states at that time, laws made it a crime for black people to use the same restaurants, schools and even sections of public transport, as white people.

King became a Baptist minister, and in his church spoke out against segregation and racism. But in 1955, something happened which led to a far greater role for him in fighting racial injustice. A woman called Rosa Parks in Montgomery, Alabama, refused to move for a white woman on a bus and was arrested. From that moment onwards, King became a leader of his people across the nation.

His first step was leading a bus boycott in Montgomery which successfully led to a change in the law about segregated seating. He went on to lead other blacks in a campaign for freedom. This included sit-ins at segregated lunch counters, demonstrations, rallies and freedom rides (bus rides to places where there were particular racial problems). The largest rally was on 28 August 1963, when 200 000 people marched together through Washington, DC.

King became well-known for his powers of oratory. When he spoke, people listened. His words at the Washington rally still have the power to stir our hearts and minds: 'I have a dream that one day this nation will rise up and live out the true meaning of its creed: We hold these truths to be self-evident that all men are created equal …'.

King's success was in part to do with his non-violent approach. Because of this, he had support from both blacks and whites. In 1963 he was named *Time Magazine*'s Man of the Year and in 1964 he received the Nobel Peace Prize.

In 1968 King was in Memphis, Tennessee, supporting striking sanitation workers. There, on 4 April, he was shot dead by James Earl Ray, a white ex-convict.

King's assassination rocked the nation and the world. Black and white people alike mourned the loss of this brilliant, courageous man who devoted his life to his people and his country, and who had the power to move an audience like no other.

LANGUAGE FEATURES

formal language

mostly objective language but may be some subjective language which shows writer's attitude to person

time phrases show chronological sequence of events, e.g. 'in 1955'

focus on specific people and events

pronouns to link ideas through text, e.g. 'he', 'his'

past tense, e.g. 'was born', 'became'

Comprehension

Understanding biographies has a lot to do with being able to follow when and where things happened. A good writer helps readers by organising information into paragraphs and by the use of specific dates and locations. As readers, we need to pay attention to this information and structure if we want to fully understand the text.

1 Underline the correct answer. The purpose of the text is to:

a tell the story of Martin Luther King's life

b explain why Martin Luther King was a great leader

c express an opinion about Martin Luther King

2 The writer uses separate paragraphs for different parts of King's life. In which paragraph (2–7) does she focus on the following?

a the start of his national involvement ____________

b his approach ____________

c his background ____________

d his achievements ____________

e his death ____________

f his powers as a speaker ____________

3 Answer these questions.

a What incident prompted King to get more involved in the civil rights movement? ____________________

____

b What did King do about this incident? ____________________

c What happened as a result of his actions? ____________________

d Where did he give his famous 'I have a dream' speech? ____________________

e What was one reason he appealed to whites as well as blacks? ____________________

4 On your own paper, draw a time-line of King's life based on information in the biography.

Writing skills

1 The writer uses the past tense to tell the story of King. Underline all the past tense verbs in the text. Why is this?

____

As said above, details about time and place are important in a biography. An important part of writing a biography is to decide about **content**—just how much detail to use: too much and the readers may be overwhelmed, too little and they may get lost.

One way to give a clear sense of time is to use **time connectives** such as *firstly*, *afterwards*, *eventually*, *then*, *finally* and *beforehand*. It is important to think carefully about the best time connectives to use and to vary them across your text. The connective *then* is an especially overused word.

2 Underline all the time phrases that the writer uses to move the biography from one chronological point to another.

3 Circle all the place phrases used in the text.

4 Most of the text is objective and factual but the writer shows her attitude to Martin Luther King in a few places. Underline the sentences in the text where this occurs. Look especially at paragraphs 1, 5 and 8.

5 The three sentences below were in the first draft of this essay, but the writer omitted them in the final draft. Why do you think the writer did this?

a *My favourite part of his 'I have a dream' speech is when he talks about his four little children.*

b *Another famous black leader was Malcolm X.*

c *It was incredibly sad when he died.*

____

____

____

Vocabulary

civil	**racism**	**tragically**	**segregation**	**injustice**
arrested	**boycott**	**successfully**	**campaign**	**rally**
racial	**oratory**	**stir**	**creed**	**self-evident**
received	**assassination**	**mourned**	**brilliant**	**courageous**

1 Put the words under the correct heading. Use the Look, Cover, Write, Check method to learn any spellings you are not sure of.

Nouns	Verbs	Adjectives	Adverbs

Most people have some trouble with words with double letters. Sometimes there is a rule or pattern that helps. For example, *~al* + *~ly* gives you double 'l' (*tragically*, *successfully*) or double letters to give you a short sound, e.g. *assassination*, *brilliant*, *rally*. Memory tricks can sometimes help, but it is not always easy and practice and memorising are generally the best methods.

2 Cover up the words above. Now test yourself by choosing the correct spelling in the following sets.

a arested, arrested, arrestted

b boycott, boycot, boyycot

c assassination, assasination, asassination

d sucessfully, succesfuly, successfully

e briliant, brillant, brilliant

Focus on punctuation

Commas

- We use **commas** to help make our meaning clear. Sometimes you hear the advice that you should put commas where you need to take a breath, but this is not always so. Doing this can break up the rhythm of your sentence and even confuse your reader.
- One way to develop your judgement of when to use commas is to study how other people use them. Take notice of how they use commas to help you understand their writing.

Decide where you would put commas in these paragraphs from 'Martin Luther King'. Then check against the text itself. Think about why the writer used the commas the way she did.

1 King was born in 1929 in Atlanta Georgia in the deep south of the USA where the segregation of black people and white people was a way of life. In most southern states at that time laws made it a crime for black people to use the same restaurants schools and even sections of public transport as white people.

2 King became a Baptist minister and in his church spoke out against segregation and racism. But in 1955 something happened which led to a far greater role for him in fighting racial injustice. A woman called Rosa Parks in Montgomery Alabama refused to move for a white woman on a bus and was arrested. From that moment onwards King became a leader of his people across the nation.

3 In 1968 King was in Memphis Tennessee supporting striking sanitation workers. There on 4 April he was shot dead by James Earl Ray a white ex-convict.

Select a word

Choose words from the vocabulary list that mean the same as these words.

1 refusal to buy or use products/services as a protest ________________

2 demonstration ________________

3 giving powerful and effective speeches in public ________________

4 move emotionally ________________

5 belief ________________

6 keeping apart, especially sexes or races ________________

7 killing of a famous/important person for political reasons ________________

8 relating to ordinary people ________________

Grammar

Cohesion—using pronouns to link ideas

- Cohesion is the way we link information and ideas in a text so that our readers can follow them.
- One way we achieve cohesion is by using **pronouns** such as *he, she, they, it, this, these* and other words such as *there, here, such* to refer back or forward to people, places, events and ideas in the text, e.g.

Martin Luther King was the leader of the Civil Rights Movement ... Tragically, at the age of 39 he was shot dead.

King became a Baptist minister, and in his church spoke out against segregation and racism.

King became well-known for his powers of oratory. When he spoke, people listened.

1 In these sentences from the text, draw a line from each underlined word to the word or words it refers to (as in the examples above).

a King was born in 1929 in Atlanta, Georgia, in the deep south of the USA, where the segregation of black people and white people was a way of life. In most southern states at that time, laws made it a crime ...

b He went on to lead other blacks in a campaign for freedom. This included sit-ins at segregated lunch counters, demonstrations, rallies and freedom rides ...

c King's success was in part to do with his non-violent approach. Because of <u>this</u>, he had support from both blacks and whites.

d In 1968 King was in Memphis, Tennessee, supporting striking sanitation workers. <u>There</u>, on 4 April, he was shot dead by James Earl Ray, a white ex-convict.

2 In the text below, choose words from the brackets to fill in the spaces and make the text cohesive.

Eddie Mabo was born in 1936 on Mer (Murray) Island in the Torres Strait. The government of Queensland controlled the island through __________ (its, his) Island Council and because of a prank during his teenage years, __________ (they, he) was exiled to the mainland. His sense of land was reinforced by __________ (their, this) experience and by his learning during __________ (his, this) time. In the sixties and seventies he worked as a gardener at James Cook University. He used __________ (this, these) time to attend lectures and read books. It was __________ (this, there) that he learned that his people did not own the island __________ (he, they) had lived on for centuries.

Subsequently, in 1981, Eddie made a speech about land ownership. __________ (This, They) sparked off a historic series of events to challenge the notion of 'terra nullius'—no man's land—which had been the basis of possession by the British in 1788. The first court battle was lost and, sadly, Eddie died of cancer in 1992, not knowing that only months later the court's decision was overturned and 'native title' was legitimised. Eddie's name is immortalised in the name of the decision and for __________ (its, his) bravery, intelligence and passion for his people and his land.

Word study

We make many words by adding **suffixes** (word endings). For example, we add *~ism* to make new words meaning beliefs or ways of behaving, e.g. *racism*. We add *~ist* to make words meaning people who have certain beliefs or behaviours, e.g. *racist*.

Add these suffixes to the words below to make new words. You may be able to make more than one word. You may have to make a change to the spelling of the original word. Use your own paper.

~ist ~ism ~age ~ness ~ance ~ence ~ment ~ity ~ee ~al

feminine	social	national	disappoint	consumer	economy	perform
prefer	sincere	interview	break	approve	waste	

Evaluating other people's writing

What is wrong with the following biography? Mark at least five things in the biography that could be improved, e.g.

- order and clarity of information and ideas
- language, e.g. formal/informal
- vocabulary and grammar
- punctuation
- the introduction

Albert Einstein was born in Germany, but when he grew up he moved to Switzerland, because it was a more peaceful country he said. He developed the theory of relativity to explain energy, and we remember him for this today.

This theory is very complicated and only a few people in the world understand the mathematics in the theory. He became a professor of physics in 1905. Teaching at the University of Zurich. He won the Nobel Prize in physics a bit later on. Einstein was good at playing the violin too.

During the second world war, his home was destroyed by the Nazis and so he did not go back there from England where he was at the time. He moved to the United States, he worked at a university. In the Second World War, scientists in America developed the atomic bomb. Although Einstein did not work on it, it was his theory that made it possible and his idea to start bomb research. When he saw what it could do he was horrified at what it did, so worked for peace after that. He was a very important man in science.

Quick think

Match these people to the reasons they are famous.

1	Neil Armstrong	a	First Nations Australian poet and activist
2	Anne Frank	b	invented penicillin, the first antibiotic
3	Cathy Freeman	c	great Indian leader who fought for freedom and peace
4	Amelia Earhart	d	first woman to fly across the Atlantic alone
5	Thomas Edison	e	great black athlete who won four gold medals at Berlin Olympics
6	Mahatma Gandhi	f	archaeologist who discovered tomb of Tutankhamen
7	Jesse Owens	g	invented the electric light bulb
8	Oodgeroo Noonuccal	h	First Nations Australian Olympic athlete
9	Howard Carter	i	wrote a diary about hiding in Amsterdam attic in World War II
10	Alexander Fleming	j	first man on the moon

Proofreading

Put full stops, capitals and commas where needed in this paragraph.

charles dickens was born in portsmouth on 7 february 1812 he grew up in great poverty when he was 12 years of age he was sent to work in a boot-blacking factory on the banks of the river thames in london his miserable time there although brief was to remain in his memory all his life he continued to work there when his father was sent to prison because of his debts it was customary in those days for whole families to go to prison with their fathers and this is what happened in Charles' father's case it was a very low and lonely point in young Charles' life.

Writing paragraphs and whole texts

1 Use the time phrases in the box to complete the biography on the next page.

on the second voyage	at the age of only 13	a month earlier	on the the return journey
11 years later	in 1906	on 17 January 1912	a year later

Robert Falcon Scott, or Scott of the Antarctic as he is often called, was born in 1868. He began his career as an explorer at the age of 33. His tragic death, **a** ______________________, is perhaps the most famous episode in polar exploration.

In 1881, **b** ______________________ he joined the navy. He was promoted to captain **c** ______________________. He led two expeditions to the Antarctic. **d** ______________________, begun in 1910, he and his companions reached the South Pole. **e** ______________________, they unfurled the Union Jack flag at the pole but, unfortunately, there was already another flag there—the flag of Norway placed there by Roald Amundsen, who had got there **f** ______________________.

g ______________________, tragedy struck, when the party was forced to stop because of a terrible blizzard. All the men were already sick with scurvy, frostbite and exhaustion. Sadly, one by one they died. Scott recorded his last hours in his diary:

'Every day now we have been ready to start for our depot 11 miles away, but outside the door of the tent, it remains a scene of whirling drift. I do not think we can hope for any better things now. We shall stick it to the end, but we are getting weaker of course ... It seems a pity, but I do not think I can write more. For God's sake look after our people.'

His diary was found and **h** ______________________, in 1913, it was published as 'Scott's Last Expedition'.

2 Use this information and timeline of the life of Mother Teresa to write a short biography. You do not need to use all the information and you may want to add information of your own. Use the space below and opposite for planning and drafting.

Born: 26 August 1910 of Albanian parents in Shkup (now called Skopje, now part of Macedonia), real name Agnes Gonxha Bojaxhiu
1927: father murdered
1928: joined convent in Ireland, 18 years old
1929: sent to Darjeeling, India
1931: began teaching at a Calcutta girls' school
1948: left teaching to work among the poor in slums of Calcutta, left order of nuns to start her own order
1950s to 1990s: worked with poor and sick, special love for children
1979: won Nobel Peace Prize
Died: 5 September 1997

3 Choose a famous person whose life interests you. Find out what you can about him or her and, on your own paper, write a biography using the texts in this chapter as your models. Use the space below for notes and planning.

CHAPTER 11

Speech

STRUCTURE

overall structure reflects text purpose—to persuade

opening, which quickly catches the audience's attention, and at the same time establishes the topic and purpose of speech

ideas organised as appropriate to purpose of speech—here arguments to support point of view

ideas not always fully developed as in an essay—because of time limits and need to limit amount of detail for audience

conclusion:

- *relates to the content and purpose of speech*
- *may include a question, a warning, a quotation*

If we kill the killer, we too deserve to be killed. Good morning class. Capital punishment. Once again, after another horrific crime, this topic is back under discussion. So, should we reintroduce it or not?
I think not.

To execute someone for a crime is to follow the ancient custom of 'an eye for an eye and a tooth for a tooth'. In other words, it is pure revenge. Think for a moment what sort of example this sets for the community at large. What does it say to them about dealing with conflict and hardship? A good message would you say?

Even if there is no doubt that someone has murdered, should the state stoop to that level and murder as well? If a convicted murderer is sentenced to life imprisonment, that person is no longer a danger to society. There is absolutely no need to execute criminals to punish them. Imprisonment is punishment enough. And imprisonment offers the hope of rehabilitation—surely something <u>we</u> should be aiming for.

Capital punishment is certainly not a deterrent. People who commit serious crimes don't think about the consequences before doing so. In the US, where capital punishment exists in some states, the murder rate is still climbing. Britain has abolished the death penalty, as has Australia, and our murder statistics per head of population are lower than in those US states. <u>Considerably lower</u>.

The death penalty is a <u>cop out</u> for dealing with our social problems. A quick fix. The roots of crime lie in poverty, abuse, racism, injustice. Society needs to look at these causes and deal with them. People who commit vicious crimes have often suffered from neglect, cruelty, emotional trauma, violence, abandonment, lack of love and a host of destructive social conditions. Is it fair to hold these people fully accountable for their wrongdoing? <u>Is not society at least partly to blame</u>?

It is not capital punishment that will make society safe from violent crime but attention to its needs. Killing will not stop crime. Caring will. Let us show mercy even to those who have shown none, to return good for evil. For to err is human, to forgive, divine.

Capital punishment is inhuman, <u>barbaric</u> and, in my eyes at least, legalised murder.

Alli Barnard

LANGUAGE FEATURES

address the audience, e.g. 'ladies and gentlemen', 'class'

more repetition and restatement of ideas than in writing—to help your listeners follow the ideas

personal language, e.g. 'I', 'you', 'we', 'us'

not always full sentences—phrases and isolated words used for effect

often some colloquial, everyday language, e.g. 'cop out'

use of rhetorical questions to set up a conversation with listeners

subjective language, e.g. 'barbaric'

Comprehension

Of course speeches are spoken texts and are created to be listened to, not to be read. However, here we will treat the text as a written text to make you more aware of its content and structure.

1 What is the speaker's main purpose? Underline the correct answer.

- **a** to inform the audience
- **b** to entertain the audience
- **c** to persuade the audience to a point of view

2 Is the speaker speaking for or against capital punishment? ______________________

Which words in the opening paragraph tell you this? _

3 The speaker has organised her ideas into five body paragraphs—each one containing one main argument to support her view. Tick which of the following main arguments the speaker uses.

- **a** Capital punishment is revenge. ______
- **b** Capital punishment sends a bad message to the community. ______
- **c** Capital punishment is not necessary as punishment. ______
- **d** Capital punishment does not stop people committing crimes. ______
- **e** The murder rate is climbing in US states with the death penalty. ______
- **f** Capital punishment is not supported by most of the community. ______
- **g** Capital punishment does not address the social problems that cause crime. ______
- **h** Capital punishment leads to further crime. ______
- **i** We should show mercy to criminals. ______

4 Use the context to work out what these expressions mean:

- **a** an eye for an eye and a tooth for a tooth
- **b** to err is human, to forgive, divine

____

____

5 Why is there no need for capital punishment, according to the speaker?

____

____

6 What evidence does the speaker give to prove that the death penalty does not stop criminals? Underline the correct answer.

- **a** comparison of the murder rate in the US and in Britain and Australia
- **b** comparison of the murder rate in US states with the death penalty and in those without it
- **c** the number of people who have been executed in the US

7 Many good speeches have an overriding idea that embodies all other points. Which of the following statements captures the speaker's main idea?

- **a** Capital punishment does not work.
- **b** Capital punishment is murder.
- **c** Capital punishment is unfair.

Writing skills

The **opening 'paragraph'** of a speech is extremely important. The speaker needs to immediately capture the audience's attention and make them want to sit up and listen to what he or she has to say.

1 Tick which of these techniques the speaker uses to catch the audience's attention in the opening paragraph.

a questions to the audience ______ **b** short, 'sharp' groups of words ______

c repetition of the same idea in different words ______ **d** reference to the audience's experience ______

e a statement that makes the audience think ______ **f** use of an interesting statistic ______

The speaker asks the audience many questions in her speech but she does not expect an answer to them. These kinds of questions are called **rhetorical questions**.

The purpose of these questions is to engage the audience and set up a kind of conversation with them. But they have another purpose too. The speaker wants the audience to think about the questions and come to the same conclusions as the speaker about the answers.

Warning: rhetorical questions can be very effective, but it is best not to overdo them.

2 The speaker asks questions in order to 'engage' the audience and set up a kind of 'conversation' with them.

a Underline all the rhetorical questions asked.

b Where could you put the following rhetorical question into the capital punishment speech?
Do you really want to have murder on your conscience?

____

Do you think this question improves the speech or not? Why?

____

3 When delivering a speech, it is important to think about where you would pause. You might pause to give your listeners:

- a signal that you are moving to another main part of the talk
- time to keep up with your ideas
- time to respond (e.g. to a controversial idea)
- time to think about what you are saying or asking

Look through the talk and mark the places where you think the speaker would pause for a second or two.

Vocabulary

horrific	**revenge**	**stoop**	**absolutely**	**rehabilitation**
deterrent	**serious**	**consequences**	**abolished**	**poverty**
abuse	**vicious**	**neglect**	**cruelty**	**trauma**
abandonment	**host**	**accountable**	**err**	**barbaric**

Write out the words in the above list and underline the parts that you think most difficult to spell, e.g. the double 'r' in *horrific* and *deterrent* may be difficult to remember, or the 'c' in *vicious*.

Now write them out again using the Look, Cover, Write, Check method.

____

____

____

____

Focus on punctuation

Punctuating speeches

Correct punctuation is not so important when writing a speech, as you are usually only writing it for yourself. However, using appropriate punctuation can help you to deliver the speech effectively, e.g. to mark where you will be asking a question, where you will be pausing for breath, and how you will break up the ideas as you talk.

Here is a part of the speech without punctuation. Punctuate it in a way that would help you deliver it effectively. (There is more than one way to punctuate it.) Then check the original text.

If we kill the killer we too deserve to be killed good morning class capital punishment once again after another horrific crime this topic is back under discussion so should we reintroduce it or not I think not

To execute someone for a crime is to follow the ancient custom of an eye for an eye and a tooth for a tooth in other words it is pure revenge think for a moment what sort of example this sets for the community at large what does it say to them about dealing with conflict and hardship a good message would you say

Select a word

Choose words from the vocabulary list that have similar meanings to these words.

1 make a mistake ________________

2 did away with, put an end to ________________

3 a bad experience that has a lasting effect ________________

4 lower yourself ________________

5 a great number ________________

6 very cruel or harmful ________________

7 something that stops you doing something ________________

8 responsible ________________

Grammar

Spoken and written language

- We speak differently from the way we write.
- In **speaking** we usually take more words to say what we mean—we spread out the words that contain the information (e.g. nouns). Speech is temporary—the words fly out in a rush and so our listeners have to understand it as it comes out.
- In **writing** we pack in the information words more tightly. We can do this because writing is permanent. The words remain still on the page. So we can take our time reading them.
- In speech we generally:
  - break up the information into short chunks
  - avoid overloading our listeners with information and ideas
  - use **concrete**, everyday words (e.g. *find*) in place of formal and **abstract** words (e.g. *locate*)
  - use personal instead of impersonal language (e.g. *we, should we*)
  - use verbs (e.g. *develop*) instead of nouns (e.g. *development*)
  - ask questions of our audience.

Below are pairs of sentences with similar meanings. Underline the sentence in each pair that is more likely to be from a speech.

1 **a** Freedom of speech is a right.
b People should be able to speak freely.

2 **a** The abolition of the death penalty has not led to a sudden increase in crime.
b When the death penalty was abolished, crime did not suddenly increase.

3 **a** We are to blame.
b Society bears the responsibility.

4 **a** Do you really think that criminals think about getting caught?
b Punishment is not a strong deterrent to criminal activity.

Word study

Find the pairs of words with opposite meanings.

illegal	introduce	acquit	guilty	abolish	imprison	poverty	wealth
abundance	legal	prohibited	convict	innocent	lack	permitted	release

Evaluating other people's writing

What could be improved in the speech on capital punishment below? Mark at least five things that could be improved, e.g.

- opening
- purpose
- organisation of ideas
- techniques to engage the audience
- vocabulary and grammar

Capital punishment means the same as the death penalty. Australia does not have the death penalty any more, but many countries do, even the United States, although not all states.

There are many reasons to use the death penalty and I will discuss some of these, but there are also reasons not to have it. Imagine if for example they convicted the wrong person and then later found out that he was innocent. The government would then be murderers.

The best reason to use capital punishment is to make the community safer. I think that most criminals would think twice about committing a violent crime if they knew that they would be executed. Wouldn't you?

I also believe that such criminals deserve to die. If they have taken a life then their life should be taken also. I know that some criminals have had very hard lives but that does not mean that they can kill people. They know what they are doing.

This is why I think that we should have the death penalty.

Quick think

Below are some tips on public speaking, but a few points are incorrect. Underline the incorrect points of advice.

Tips for public speaking

- Write your points on small cards.
- Make eye contact with only one person in the audience.
- Use facial and body gestures.
- Stand still and straight.
- Speak slowly, clearly and loudly.
- Always be serious.
- Vary your tone of voice, and your speed of delivery
- Try to memorise your whole speech.
- Don't sway or walk around the stage.
- Imagine you are speaking to the person furthest away.
- Don't touch your hair, scratch your face etc.
- Remember to pause frequently to give your audience time to catch up.

Proofreading

Which words are spelt incorrectly? Correct any mistakes you find, and then check your corrections against the chapter spelling list.

horific	revege	stoop	absolutly	rehabilation
deterent	serios	consequences	abolished	povety
abuse	visious	neglect	crulty	truama
abandnment	host	accountable	err	barbaric

Writing paragraphs and whole texts

1 Here are some points about the death penalty:

- Many people think the death penalty deters people from committing murder but evidence does not show this.
- Some US states that have the death penalty have higher homicide rates than states that do not.
- When US states abolished the death penalty homicide rates did not go up.
- In US states that have the death penalty, homicide rates do not decline when there is an execution.
- The death penalty does not deter murderers, because murder is a usually a crime of passion, carried out in extreme fits of emotion and uncontrollable rage.
- Capital punishment satisfies the sense of outrage in the community.
- One survey showed that more than half of the US adult population would still favour capital punishment even if they knew that it did not deter murder.
- The US is the only industrialised nation that still executes murderers, and it still has the highest murder rate in the industrialised world.

Choose from these points to write one or two paragraphs you could use in a speech about capital punishment (on either side of the argument). Do not just use the words above. Add your own words to them to make them interesting to your audience.

Remember:

- Do not try to say too much.
- Change some of the information into more spoken language, e.g. make into questions, use personal language.
- Keep your sentences quite short so that it is easy for your listeners to follow you.

Use the space below for your notes and drafting.

2 **a** Read these notes made to prepare for a speech about the future of books in our society. Underline which you would use in a 2-minute speech on the topic.

- *Can't read an electronic book in bed or in the bath*
- *Most people like reading books.*
- *What about children's books?*
- *We will run out of trees soon.*
- *Not everyone will be able to afford the new technology.*
- *Television is better than reading.*
- *Technology will make books unnecessary.*
- *Scrolls were used before books were invented.*
- *Books feel nice to hold and touch.*
- *Many people hate computers.*

b Think about how you would begin your speech to quickly establish your topic and purpose. For example, you might:

- ask the audience a question
- say something that you know the audience will relate to
- quickly create an image (short, sharp, interesting).

Write your introduction (no more than a few sentences). Use the space below.

c Now write the rest of the speech in the space below. Your information and ideas will depend on your purpose. You might, for example:

- discuss arguments for and against
- argue for one view
- entertain listeners with imaginative, humorous ideas about computerised books.

3 Write a short speech, using your own paper, on a topic that you are interested in. You could use the texts in this book to give you ideas.

CHAPTER 12

Advertisement

STRUCTURE

overall structure reflects dual purpose—to inform and persuade

visuals to attract readers' attention

important words in largest letters

layout features, e.g. bold to highlight information

enough information to attract and inform readers but not too much

only important information included because of limited space

no single way to organise information—depends on purpose of advertisement and practical aspects such as space available

contact numbers usually at end

Advertisement A

Young Women needed to form Music Groups

♮Are you interested in music?
♮Do you play an instrument?
♮Do you have material you would like to produce?
♮Do you write your own songs?

We are running a 6-week program for young female musicians. You will be tutored in different aspects of the music industry. We will provide you with an opportunity to form a band/group and perform for members of the community. At the end of the program you will receive your own compilation CD to keep.

The program starts on Saturday 3rd July 10 am–4 pm at Winmalee Youth Service, Whitecross Rd, Winmalee. Workshops are free. Lunch provided.

Contact Kate at Winmalee Youth Service on (02) 4754-5125 or Horace at Springwood Youth Project on (02) 4751-1005.

T386/W26

Advertisement B

Wearable
BODY ART *Workshops*

A series of free workshops for all young people (12–24) interested in costume, design, sculpture, mask, techno-party wear and the performance arts will be hosted by Springwood Youth Project, starting 9 July. Materials and munchies provided. Bookings are essential.

(02) 4751-1005

T385/W26

LANGUAGE FEATURES

often questions to engage reader

words chosen to suit target audience (e.g. young people)

not always complete sentences, e.g. 'Lunch provided.'

choice of language very much dependent on space (and cost) requirements

Comprehension

Advertisements are usually quite easy to understand—they do not have as many words as other texts and they make good use of visuals and layout. Nevertheless, we, as readers, still have to read them closely to be sure we have understood the main purpose, audience and information.

1 Underline what is being advertised in Advertisement A.

a musical instruments **b** a job in the music industry **c** a training program

2 Underline what is being advertised in Advertisement B.

a workshops **b** an exhibition **c** costumes and other art for sale

3 Who is the target audience of:

a Advertisement A ____________________ **b** Advertisement B ____________________

4 What audience do you think Advertisement A is mainly targeting (circle one)?

a readers in lower secondary school **b** readers in upper secondary school

c readers who have left school **d** a and b

e b and c

Which words give you this impression?

5 Name two special attractions of what is being advertised in:

a Advertisement A **b** Advertisement B

____

Writing skills

Writing advertisements looks easy. However, it can be as hard to write something 'short and sweet' as it is to write something long like an essay. It can take lots of drafting and revising to get an advertisement right, especially if there is limited space. Choice of words and clarity are all-important. There should be a very good reason for every single word used—if there isn't, the word may need to go.

1 List at least two similarities between Advertisements A and B.

____

2 List at least two differences between Advertisements A and B.

____

3 Which advertisement (A or B) do you think is the most effective in attracting the attention of the potential target audience? Why?

____

____

4 Advertisement A uses questions to engage the target audience. Write two or three similar questions to engage the target audience of Advertisement B.

____

____

5 Imagine that the writer of Advertisement A has to reduce the number of words because of space and cost. She decides to convert the section from *We are running* ... to ... *CD to keep*. to bullet points. She begins this way:

- 6-week program for young female musicians
- different aspects of music industry covered

Can you finish the bullet point conversion for her?

____

____

____

6 List some differences between this advertisement (right) and Advertisements A and B.

____

____

____

Vocabulary

instrument	**material**	**produce**	**musicians**	**tutored**
aspects	**provide**	**opportunity**	**community**	**receive**
compilation	**wearable**	**series**	**interested**	**costume**
design	**sculpture**	**hosted**	**munchies**	**essential**

Words that use 'ie' or 'ei' for the 'ee' sound can be tricky to remember. However, there are not many words that use these letters for the 'ee' sound. In general, the rule is 'i' before 'e' except after 'c', or except if the sound is a long 'a':

so *believe*, *retrieve* but *receive*, *ceiling*, *deceive*, *deceit*, and *veil*, *eight*, *weigh*, *neighbour*

The best way to remember whether to use 'ei' or 'ie' is to find a way to memorise the word itself.

Learn the words in the list using the Look, Cover, Write, Check method.

1 Cover up the words above. Now test yourself by choosing which of the following word sets are correctly spelled.

a aspects, interested, musicians, esential
b aspexts, intersted, musiciens, essential
c aspects, interested, musicens, essensial
d aspects, interested, musicians, essential
e aspects, intrested, musicians, essentiel

2 Now choose the correctly spelled set of these below.

a receive, tutored, opportunity, material
b receive, tutered, oportunity, material
c receve, tutored, oportunity, material
d receive, tutored, opportunty, matireal
e recieve, tutored, opportunity, material

Focus on punctuation

Punctuating advertisements

Just like any other text, advertisements need punctuation to get their meaning across clearly and effectively. This is so whether they are written for newspapers, magazines, notice-boards or online sites. However, the rules are a little more relaxed than for other texts.

Generally, in advertisements we:

- use full stops and commas less than we would in other writing, because we do not want to clutter up the space
- use question marks as usual because it is usually important for questions to stand out
- use capitals more than we would in other writing, to emphasise important information and ideas, e.g. *Workshops are Free*, or even all capitals, e.g. *BOOK NOW*
- use other punctuation as needed, e.g. dashes (—) , exclamation marks (!)

Punctuate this advertisement as needed.

bored
feel like some interesting holiday action
ever tried snorkelling
explore the fascinating world under the sea you'll love it
individuals small groups or large groups
safe for kids
two-hour half-day or whole-day trips
$15 an hour concessions available
we provide wetsuits and all other gear you need
ring jai or anika (02) 6899 9999—now

Select a word

Choose words from the vocabulary list that have the same meanings as these words.

1 substance, raw matter from which a thing is made or composed ______________

2 features, parts ______________

3 organised; space and other things provided ______________

4 necessary ______________

5 light food (not full meals) ______________

6 taught ______________

7 collection of songs or other material from different sources ______________

8 able to be worn on the body ______________

Grammar

Leaving out words (ellipsis)

- In advertisements we often give the meaning of full sentences without using all the words.
- We leave out the words that we know will not affect understanding—the words that the reader can easily recognise as missing, e.g.
  Lunch provided. (meaning: *Lunch will be provided.*)
  Interested in music? (meaning: *Are you interested in music?*)
- When we leave out words like this, it is called an **ellipsis**. It is important when leaving out words that we do not interfere with the grammar of the sentence. For example, instead of using the words *the project has been praised* we could write *project praised*, but we could not write *project has praised.*
- The types of words we leave out are:
  - part of the verb (*has been, is*)
  - pronouns (*you, we*)
  - less important content words (adjectives, adverbs)
  - small function words such as *from, for, when, to, the*
- We use the ellipsis in all kinds of writing—not only advertisements. For example, we write:
  The boys ran hard and finally caught up with the thief

  instead of
  The boys ran hard and the boys finally caught up with the thief.

1 Write out the full meanings of these groups of words from advertisements.

a lessons half-hour or one-hour ______________________

b afternoon teas available from 4 ______________________

c bookings a must—members free, non-members $10 ______________________

d opposite station ______________________

2 Write these sentences in short form.

a The play is ideal holiday entertainment for children under 10 years of age.

b There are concessions for schoolchildren.

c You need to book now or you will miss out.

d All ages are welcome to attend, but the course is especially suitable for teenagers.

____

____

3 Read the following sentence and then choose which of the sentences (a–c) uses ellipsis correctly (clear meaning and correct grammar).

The Theatresports West troupe is putting on its next dazzling show on Friday February 24 at the Victoria Theatre in Maxville.

a The Theatresports West troupe putting on next dazzling show on Friday February 24 at Victoria Theatre in Maxville.

b The Theatresports West is putting on its show on Friday, February 24 the Victoria Theatre in Maxville.

c Theatresports West next dazzling show, Friday February 24, Victoria Theatre, Maxville.

Word study

Make adjectives from these words by adding the endings *~al, ~able, ~ible, ~ive, ~ic, ~ful,* e.g. music—musical. You may have to omit some letters at the end of the word.

1 instrument ____________	**2** community ____________
3 wear ____________	**4** decorate ____________
5 artist ____________	**6** region ____________
7 person ____________	**8** create ____________
9 imagination ____________	**10** skill ____________

Evaluating other people's writing

What is wrong with this advertisement? Mark at least five things that could be improved, e.g.

- layout and organisation (e.g. use of bold, CAPITAL LETTERS, underlining etc.)
- punctuation
- unnecessary words

PRINTMAKING STUDIO CLASSES
LEARN THE ART OF PRINTMAKING IN A SMALL FRIENDLY STUDIO ENVIRONMENT
Produce works on paper or fabric.
We work in small groups but we can also offer individualised tuition.
You do not need your own equipment. We will supply everything you need.
The classes run for 6 weeks—that's 18 hours in all. The cost is $130.
I am a qualified teacher and practising artist. I have taught printmaking for the past 6 years.
Please ring me on 0265111111.

Quick think

Music*ians* are people who play music. What people do these things? Add *~er, ~or, ~ist, or ~ian.*

1 edit ____________	**2** direct ____________
3 drive ____________	**4** produce ____________
5 design ____________	**6** act ____________
7 govern ____________	**8** study history ____________
9 juggle ____________	**10** do mathematics ____________
11 sculpt ____________	**12** play piano ____________

Proofreading

Which words are spelt incorrectly? Correct any mistakes you find and then check your corrections against the chapter vocabulary list.

instrement	materiel	produse	musicians	tutored
aspects	provide	oportunity	community	recieve
compilation	wearible	seres	intrested	costume
desine	scupture	hosted	munchies	esential

Writing paragraphs and whole texts

1 Convert this short newspaper article into an advertisement. Only use the important information. Use layout and punctuation to emphasise some important words and change the order of information if you need to.

Art and craft show

Nepean High School will hold its art and craft show on Friday, Saturday and Sunday, October 15, 16 and 17.

Kylie Watson, who plays Shauna Bradley in 'Home and Away', will officially open the art show on the Friday night at 7.30 pm. It will be open from 9 am to 6 pm on the Saturday, and from 9 am to 4 pm on the Sunday.

The work of Blue Mountains artist Fay Graham will feature in the art show. The high school is located on the Great Western Highway at Emu Plains.

Blue Mountains Gazette, 29 September, p. 44

2 Do the same with this newspaper advertisement. Include some information about the Young Textile and Fibre Group as well as the display itself, using the space on the next page.

Young textile and fibre artists at Braemar

A colourful display of embroidery by the Young Textile and Fibre Group of the Embroiderers' Guild, NSW Inc. will be officially opened by Councillor Angelique Henson at 10 am on Saturday, October 9.

The display, which will run from Saturday, October 2 to Sunday, October 24, will showcase works created by young artists from 5 to 18 years old.

The works on show will reflect the Young Textile and Fibre Group's aim to encourage the use of textiles in mixed media and fibre techniques, creative skills and free and imaginative expression using individual ideas and designs.

Braemar Gallery, 104 Macquarie Road, Springwood, is open Friday to Sunday from 10 am to 4 pm, or by arrangement outside hours.

3 Write an advertisement for some activity you know about or are involved in. It might be, for example, a school performance, a course or program, or a sports event. Think about these things:

- What can you say to attract your audience to the advertisement and the activity being advertised?
- How can you make the most important information stand out?
- How can you fit the interesting or important details into the space?
- What visuals could you use to attract the audience to the advertisement?

Use the space below for your planning and drafting.

CHAPTER 13

Explanation

STRUCTURE

overall structure reflects text purpose—to explain a process

introduction, which identifies and says something about the process being explained

focus on factual information

relevant information only

information about how or why phenomenon works—usually in the order things occur in real world

may or may not be conclusion (depends on topic and length of explanation)

The human eye

The human eye is perhaps our most important sense organ. We depend upon sight more than upon any other sense to supply us with crucial information about the world we live in.

In many ways <u>the eye</u> operates like a camera. Light rays enter through a small area of transparent material (called the cornea). The amount of light allowed in is controlled by the widening or narrowing of the pupil, which acts like a camera aperture. (The pupil is the black hole in the middle of the iris or coloured part of the eye.) The light rays are then brought into focus by the lens behind the pupil, and projected onto a membrane at the back of the eyeball. This membrane acts like the film inside the camera and is called the retina. As in a camera, the image projected is <u>inverted</u> (upside-down).

However, the similarity between a camera and the eye ends there. When we take a photo, we are just recording images onto film. Our eyes do much more than this. <u>They</u> allow us to make sense of what we see. This is because the eyes are connected to the brain. The images that are formed on the darkened back wall of the retina are converted into electrical impulses. These impulses <u>are sent</u> to the brain along the optic nerve, and are then converted into messages that are meaningful to us.

There are two particularly important things the brain does. Firstly, it puts together the separate information it receives from each eye so that we do not see double. Secondly, it learns to read the upside-down images on our retina and turn them the right way up. The brain learns to do both these things automatically when we are very young, but small babies actually do see double and upside-down for a short while.

The brain also sorts out the information it gets from the two different types of light-sensitive nerve cells on the retina—rods and cones. The rods are highly sensitive to light intensity but do not register colour. The cones <u>see</u> colour and fine details, but only <u>work</u> in bright light. This is why, when daylight begins to fade, our sight is less clear and colours disappear or become a green-grey or blue.

LANGUAGE FEATURES

formal and impersonal language

mostly generic non-human nouns, e.g. 'the eye', 'the brain', 'impulses'

technical terms, often with everyday terms to help explain them

pronouns to link ideas through text, e.g. 'it', 'they'

often passive voice, e.g. 'are sent'

repetition of key words throughout text to link ideas, e.g. 'light rays'

time and cause–effect relationships

usually present tense, e.g. 'see', 'work'

Comprehension

We need to read carefully to properly understand explanation texts. We have to understand and keep track of detailed technical information, while keeping hold of the overall process being explained. Good writers help us to do this, with good organisation of ideas and careful use of language, including technical terms.

1 Underline the correct answer. The overall purpose of the text is to:

a discuss the importance of vision **b** explain how our eyes work

c describe the different sections of the eye

2 Why is the eye so important to human beings, according to the text?

____

3 The writer compares the parts of the eye to parts of a camera. Use the text and your knowledge of cameras to fill in the parts of the eye in this chart.

Camera	Eye
viewfinder	
aperture	
lens	
film	

4 In what important way is a camera different from the human eye, according to the text?

____

5 Name the three things that the brain must do to make use of the information it receives.

____

____

____

Writing skills

Cohesion is a very important element of all good writing. As we saw in Chapter 10 (Grammar, p. 73), 'cohesion' refers to the way we link ideas and information so that our readers can follow them. In Chapter 10, we looked at the use of pronouns and words like *this*, *there* and *these* to do this.

Other cohesive devices are repetition of key words, the use of linking words such as conjunctions (see Chapter 14) and the use of words and phrases that show the overall organisation of ideas across the text, e.g. *firstly*, *secondly*, *finally*, in addition.

1 The writer of 'The human eye' uses many pronouns and other words like <u>this</u> and <u>these</u> to link ideas. What do the italicised words in the following refer to in the text?

a Our eyes do much more than *this*. (paragraph 3) ______________

b *These* impulses are sent to the brain along the optic nerve ... (paragraph 3) ______________

c ... and turn *them* the right way up. (paragraph 4) ______________

d The brain learns to do both *these* things automatically ... (paragraph 4) ______________

2 The writer also repeats some key words to help the reader follow the ideas. Count the number of times he uses these words: *eye/eyes, camera, brain.* ______________________________

3 The writer uses some important words to show the overall organisation of ideas. Read this 'mini' version of paragraphs 2 to 5 of the text and insert the missing linking words used in the text.

The eye is like a camera in many ways. ____________________, there are some important differences.

There are two important things the brain does. ____________________ it puts together information

from each eye and ____________________ it learns to read upside-down. The brain

____________________ sorts out information from two types of nerve cells.

4 The four sentences below were in the first draft of this essay, but the writer omitted them in the final draft. Why do you think the writer did this?

a *I think our eyes are more important to us than our ears, but some people may disagree.*

b *The most common sight problems are short-sightedness and long-sightedness.*

c *Humans have quite good eyesight compared to many animals.*

d *My uncle was blind from birth.*

____

____

____

5 We use the **passive voice** when we want to focus on the action (the verb) and not on the person or thing doing the action, e.g. *impulses are sent* instead of *(the retina) sends impulses*. Underline all the examples of the passive voice you can find in paragraphs 2 and 3. See the next page (Grammar) for a fuller explanation of the passive voice.

Vocabulary

organ	**supply**	**crucial**	**transparent**	**aperture**
focus	**projected**	**membrane**	**inverted**	**similarity**
converted	**impulses**	**optic**	**meaningful**	**particularly**
double	**automatically**	**sensitive**	**register**	**disappear**

Put the words under the correct headings. Use the Look, Cover, Check, Write method to learn any spellings you are not sure of.

Nouns	Verbs	Adjectives	Adverbs

Without looking back, complete the spelling of these words from the list. Check your answers against the words in the list when you have finished.

conv___ ted	d______ble	cruc___l
sens______tive	transp______ent	ap___t__re
simil______ity	partic___l_____ly	di___a______ear

Focus on punctuation

Brackets

- We use **brackets** (...) to include extra bits of information.
- Brackets are useful when we want to introduce or explain technical (or specialised) terms, but not interrupt the flow of the text or end up with a very long sentence, e.g.
  Light rays enter through a small area of transparent material (called the cornea).
  ... of the pupil, which acts like a camera aperture. (The pupil is the black hole in the middle of the iris or coloured part of the eye.)
  As in a camera, the image projected is inverted (upside-down).

Use brackets where needed in these sentences to introduce or explain the technical terms.

1. Each main part or organ of your body is made of different kinds of cells.
2. The top part of our skin called the epidermis wears away as we wash and dry ourselves and move about.
3. Waxy and oily substances are made by tiny glands called the sebaceous glands near the hair.
4. A single nerve cell or neuron is much thinner than an ordinary electrical wire.
5. One set of nerves carries signals to your brain the sensory nerves and one set of nerves carries signals from your brain to your muscles the motor nerves.

Select a word

Choose words from the vocabulary list that mean the same as these words.

1. opening ______________________
2. essential, very important ______________________
3. thin sheet of animal or vegetable tissue ______________________
4. show or indicate ______________________
5. clear ______________________
6. changed ______________________
7. stimuli conveyed by the nervous system ______________________
8. significant, having meaning ______________________

Grammar

Active and passive voice of the verb

- Verbs are either in the **active** or the **passive voice**.
- We use the **active voice** when we want the focus on who or what is doing the action (the actor), e.g.

  Human beings rely heavily on their eyes.
  The brain sorts out information.

  The person or thing being focused on is in the subject position of the sentence. (*Human beings* and *The brain* are the subjects in the above examples.)
- We use the **passive voice** when we want the focus on the thing being acted upon, or on the process described by the verb, e.g.

  The amount of light is controlled by the pupil.

  The person or thing being focused on is in the subject position of the sentence. (*The amount of light* is the subject in the above example.)
- Sometimes when we use the passive, it is not important to say who the actor is, and sometimes we may even want to avoid saying who the actor is, e.g.

  This is called the retina. (It is not important to say who calls it the retina.)

1 Identify which of these sentences are in the active voice (A) and which are in the passive voice (P). Underline the subjects of the sentences.

a X-rays were first identified by William Roentgen. ______

b The Hubble Space Telescope collects images from space. ______

c Blood circulates around the body in arteries and veins. ______

d The moon is kept in orbit by the Earth's gravity. ______

e The first jet-powered flight was made in Germany in the 1930s. ______

f Photography was not invented by any one person. ______

g The skin consists of two layers of tissue. ______

2 Change these sentences to the passive voice. (That is, make the underlined words the subjects of your sentences.) Begin your sentences with the underlined words, e.g. *Parents pass on their genes to their children.* (*Genes are passed on from parents to their children.*)

a The brain controls and coordinates the millions of signals.

____

b Muscles make up about half your weight.

____

c Blood carries oxygen to every part of the body.

____

d Every part of your body needs oxygen.

____

Word study

Opposites of many verbs are formed by adding the prefix *dis~* or *mis~*, e.g. *appear—disappear*, *understand—misunderstand*. Form opposites of these verbs by adding *dis~* or *mis~*.

1 connect ______________________ **2** behave ______________________

3 advantage ______________________ **4** understand ______________________

5 lead ______________________ **6** obey ______________________

7 approve ______________________ **8** infect ______________________

9 calculate ______________________ **10** agree ______________________

11 guide ______________________ **12** place ______________________

Evaluating other people's writing

What is wrong with the student's explanation below of how the ear works? Mark at least five things that could be improved, e.g.

- content
- vocabulary and grammar
- organisation of information
- punctuation

The part of your ear that you see is called the outer ear. This collects sound and funnels it into your ear canal. Your ear canal is about 3 or 4 centimetres inside your head—not far from your eye actually. It is brilliant the way the ear works really.

The ear is well protected because it so sensitive and has such fine bones in it. The inner ear turns sound waves into electrical impulses and these go to our brain. The brain sorts out the signals and we hear.

Having two ears is very useful because it helps us judge distance and where the sound is coming from, but one ear is better than none.

The sound goes from the outer ear which is like an ear trumpet, through the canal and onto the ear drum, it then goes past three tiny bones and through some fluid in the inner ear, then it is converted to electrical signals.

Quick think

How much do you know about the human body? Underline the correct answer.

1 There are about ______________________ bones in the adult human body.
a 200 **b** 500 **c** 50

2 An adult man has about ______________________ litres of blood in his body.
a 1–2 **b** 5–6 **c** 8–10

3 The human brain is made up of about ______________________ water.
a 50% **b** 25% **c** 80%

4 The human brain weighs about ______________________ kilograms.
a 1.4 **b** 2 **c** 4

5 Your body is approximately ______________________ water.
a 70% **b** 50% **c** 30%

Proofreading

Find the incomplete sentences in this short explanation, and add words to make them into complete sentences.

> The human brain is like a super computer. Storing millions of bits of information at the same time. It is able to recall all this information instantly. Our brain records all the information that our five senses gather. For example, our sense of sight or smell. This is why we can recognise a friend when we see him or her. Or recognise a smell after a long time. At the same time as it is collecting information, it is controlling the thousands of things that are going on in our body. It is made up almost entirely of nerve cells. Approximately 10 000 million of them.

Writing paragraphs and whole texts

1 Put these sentences into an order that explains how the heart works. Use the words in italics to help you.

- **a** *When the atrium is full,* it contracts, a valve at its inlet from the veins closes and the blood passes into the lower chamber (called *the ventricle*).
- **b** In the *upper chamber* (called the atrium), the blood collects from the veins, which bring blood from the lungs or other parts of the body.
- **c** *Each pump* has *two chambers.*
- **d** *The one on the left* pumps blood from the lungs into the body and *the one on the right* pumps blood away from the body into the lungs.
- **e** When *the ventricle* contracts, another valve closes, making sure *the blood* flows out of the chamber.
- **f** *The blood* is then pumped out into the arteries, which carry it to the lungs or around the body.
- **g** The heart is essentially *two pumps lying next to each other.*

____

2 Use the diagram to write a short explanation of how the ear works in the space below and opposite. You could also use some of the information in the text in 'Evaluating other people's writing'. Here is one way you could begin your explanation:

Sounds go through many different forms before they reach your brain.

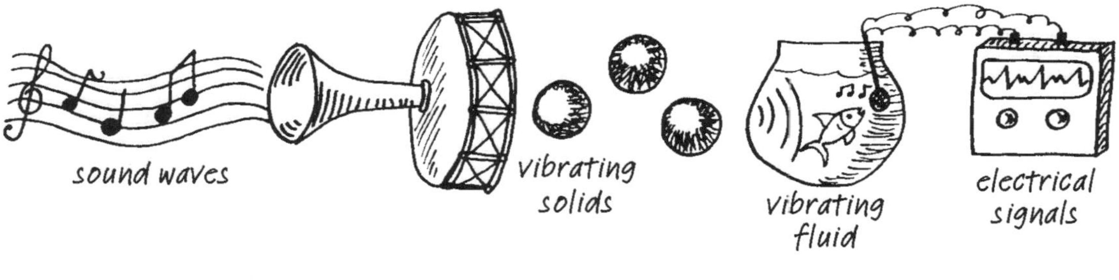

____

____

____

____

____

____

3 Write an explanation of a process you are familiar with for a reader who is not familiar with it. It could be the way something works in your school (e.g. the merit or referral system, a message system) or at home (e.g. a household routine). It could be how something works in a sport you play. Follow these steps to prepare for writing:

- Think about which information your reader needs to know, and which he/she does not need to know.
- Break up the process into the smallest parts.
- Put the parts in the correct order.
- Think about how you will introduce your subject.

Now write your explanation. And remember—the focus is on factual information. Your opinion about the process is not important. Use the space below for your notes and planning.

CHAPTER 14

Factual report

Write a report about one endangered animal. Include information about characteristics, behaviour and habitat, the reasons for its endangerment and what is being done about the problem.

The black rhino

Between about 55 and 25 million years ago, rhinoceroses were among the most dominant hoofed mammals. Today, there are only five surviving species and all are on the verge of extinction. One of these is the African black rhino, whose scientific name *Diceros bicornis* means two-horned.

The black rhino has thick, hairless, grey (not black) skin. It can grow to a length of 3.8 metres, a height of 1.7 metres and a weight of 1800 kilograms. Its front horn can grow to 1.3 metres. The rhino's upper lip is pointed or hooked in contrast to the white rhino, which has a square lip. The rhino has very poor eyesight but good hearing. However, smell is its best sense, and it uses this to detect its very few predators and other rhinos.

The black rhino lives in small pockets of eastern and southern Africa in grasslands (savannas) and woodlands. Each rhino lives in an area of its own called its home range. Some females share part of their home range but males keep clear boundaries between theirs. Rhinos mark out their land by spraying urine on paths and borders, scraping over sites with their legs and horns, and using regular dung heaps.

The International Rhino Foundation calls the endangerment of all rhinos 'a crisis of catastrophic proportions for such a venerable group of animals' (IRF website). They predict that without drastic action four species of rhino could be extinct in the wild within the next ten to twenty years. The black rhino has suffered the most spectacular decline with populations reduced by 90% in the last thirty years (African Wildlife Organisation website). The main problem is people poaching for horns to use in eastern medicines or as decorative handles for ceremonial daggers.

There have been intense antipoaching efforts over the last two decades and this had led to a stabilisation of the population at about 6000. In Zimbabwe, for example, armed rangers defend game parks. In Namibia, conservationists dehorn rhinos in a simple, painless operation so they will be valueless. Protected sanctuaries in Kenya have allowed the species to increase there by 5% each year. International captive breeding programs such as the one at the Western Plains Zoo in Dubbo, New South Wales, have also contributed. While the results of conservation programs have been encouraging, poaching remains a very real threat to the survival of the magnificent black rhino.

1. African Wildlife Organisation website: http:/www.awf.org/section/wildlife/rhinos
2. International Rhino Foundation website, http://www.rhinos-irf.org/rhinos.
3. Wildlife Factfile, 'Black Rhinoceros' & 'Save the Black Rhino', International Masters Publishers.

Hannah McLean

STRUCTURE

overall structure reflects text purpose—to present information

introduction, which defines and/or classifies topic

focus on facts, not opinion

relevant information only

paragraphs—each on a different aspect of the topic (subtopic)

(longer report may be divided into numbered sections)

may or may not be conclusion (depends on topic and length of report)

conclusion rounds off topic in some way

LANGUAGE FEATURES

formal and impersonal language

technical terms, often with an everyday term to help explain them

mostly generic nouns to refer in general to a whole group, e.g. 'rhinoceroses', 'the black rhino', 'creatures'

subject of report often the subject of clauses and sentences—to link ideas

pronouns to link ideas through text

usually present tense, e.g. 'lives'

many being and having verbs, e.g. 'is', 'has'

reference to sources

Comprehension

As with explanations (see previous chapter), we generally need to read factual reports very carefully to fully understand them. There is usually important detail (often technical) to take in as well as main ideas. Good writers help us with good organisation over the whole text and within paragraphs.

1 What does the assignment question ask the writer to do? Underline the correct answer.

a give an opinion **b** give factual information **c** discuss ideas

2 The writer could have used headings to separate the parts of the report. Where would you put these headings? Write the number of the paragraph.

Habitat ____________________ Endangerment ____________________

Conservation efforts ____________________ Characteristics ____________________

Do you think this would have helped you follow the report? ____

3 Where would you add these sentences? Mark the text with an ✗.

a These areas are primarily in Zimbabwe, Namibia, Kenya and South Africa.

b It may be inaccurately called black because of the dark-coloured local soil which often coats its skin.

c Some poachers, however, also take the skin, blood and urine of the dead rhinos because they are thought to have magical healing powers.

d In fact, this is the best way to distinguish it from the white rhino.

You often need to go back over a report or other factual text to find specific information. To do this, you need to scan—that is, to quickly run your eyes over the words until you find the right paragraph and sentence.

4 Scan the text now to find this specific information.

a How many horns does the black rhino have?

____

b What is a home range?

____

c Why do some people want to kill black rhinos?

____

d About how many black rhinos are there now?

____

e Name four methods of conservation used to protect the black rhino.

____

Writing skills

You often end up with too many facts to include in your writing after doing your research. An important part of good report writing is deciding which facts to include and how much detail is necessary for your purpose and your readers.

1 The writer manages to achieve a number of things in the short introduction. Tick them.

a tells us something about what a black rhino looks like ______

b tells us that it belongs to the rhinoceros family ______

c tells us where it is found ______

d introduces the theme of endangerment ______

e tells us the scientific name of the black rhino ______

2 Where would you put this paragraph about black rhinos (mark the text with *) and what would you call it if you had to give it a heading?

Black rhinos do not eat other creatures but instead feed on leaves, twigs and grasses. They use their front feet for digging but may unearth roots and bulbs with their horns. They use their hooked lip to strip vegetation for eating. They can survive a few days at a time without water, but during long periods of drought they may have to dig the ground to find water.

____

3 The writer uses pronouns (e.g. *it, they*) and words like *this, these* to link ideas in the text. What do the italicised words in the following sentences refer to in the text?

a it uses *this* to detect its very few predators and other rhinos (para. 2)

____

b ... but males keep clear boundaries between *theirs* (para. 3) ______________________________

c *They* predict that without drastic action four species of rhino could be extinct ... (para. 4) ______________

d ... so *they* will be valueless (para. 5) ______________________________

> In reports and explanations and other factual writing, we mostly refer in a general way to the people, animals or things we are writing about by using **generic noun** forms.
>
> We can use the plural form, e.g. *black rhinos, some females*, or the singular, e.g. *the black rhino, the female.*
>
> Whichever we use, we must be careful to use the correct forms of any pronouns or verbs to refer back to them. For example, we should write: *The rhino has poor eyesight but it has a good sense of smell*, NOT *The rhino has poor eyesight but they have a good sense of smell.*

4 Correct any errors in these sentences by writing the correct forms above each sentence.

a When a worker bee finds flowers, it tells the other bees what it has found.

b During their life, a female butterfly lays from 100 to several thousand eggs.

c Wasps take very good care of its young and travels a long way to find just the right insect to feed them.

d Crickets have keen ears, which are located on their legs instead of its heads.

e The ostrich is a strange bird with many odd things about them, but it does not hide its head in the sand.

f Because whales, like all other water mammals, are descended from ancestors who lived on the land, it has had to adapt itself to life in the water.

5 The three sentences below were in the first draft of this essay, but the writer omitted them in the final draft. Why do you think the writer did this?

a *You can become a member of the International Rhino Foundation by visiting its website.*

b *The Indian rhinoceros is one of the two greatest success stories in rhino conservation.*

c *The cruel poachers butcher the rhinos for their horns, and then just leave them to rot.*

d *I don't understand how anyone could kill such a magnificent creature.*

____

____

____

____

Vocabulary

dominant	verge	extinction	predators	boundaries
endangerment	crisis	catastrophic	proportions	venerable
drastic	spectacular	poaching	ceremonial	daggers
intense	stabilisation	sanctuaries	encouraging	magnificent

1 Remember that breaking words into syllables is an extremely important spelling strategy. Practise your syllabification skills now by writing how many syllables there are next to each word in the list.

2 Put the words under the correct heading. Use the Look, Cover, Check, Write method to learn any spellings you are not sure of.

Nouns	Verbs	Adjectives	Adverbs

Focus on punctuation

References

- Always include **references** of books or other materials you use in writing an assignment.
- Give enough information for your readers to find the information themselves.
- There are a few different ways to do this and your teacher may tell you a particular way.
- One way to reference a **book** is to give this information in this order:
  the author, the year, the name of the book, the publisher and the place of publication, e.g.
  Jones, F. (1999) *Tigers in the Wild*, Lakes Publications, Sydney
- One way to reference a **web page** is like this:
  International Rhino Foundation website (1996), http://www.rhinos-irf.org/rhinos.
  (There is not always a date on websites.)
- When you reference material in the **body of the essay** you usually write only the author, the date and the page number, e.g. Jones, 1999, p. 10.

Follow these patterns to write full references for:

- two books
- two websites

Select a word

Choose words from the vocabulary list that mean the same as these words.

1 the edge, close to the edge ____________________

2 animals that hunt, kill and eat other animals ____________________

3 more important, stronger than others of the same kind ____________________

4 size, extent ____________________

5 deserving respect because of importance ____________________

6 severe, extreme ____________________

7 safe places ____________________

8 positive, giving hope ____________________

Grammar

Conjunctions and connectives

- There are some **conjunctions** that can link two equal clauses together to create one compound sentence. These are *and*, *but*, or *or*, *nor*, *yet* and *so*.
- There are other words, generally called **connectives**, that can be used to link two equal clauses. However, if these are used, the second clause is a new sentence. Examples of these connectives are: *in addition, furthermore, moreover, that is, on the other hand, in contrast, instead, likewise, meanwhile, finally, at first, then, therefore, nevertheless, however, otherwise, so*
- So we write
  The rhino has very poor eyesight but good hearing. However, smell is its best sense ...

  But NOT
  The rhino has very poor eyesight but good hearing, however, smell is its best sense ...

  We could also use a semicolon (;) and write
  The rhino has very poor eyesight but good hearing; however, smell is its best sense ...

Look back to question 3 in the Chapter 3 'Writing paragraphs and whole texts' section for more on connectives which show time and chronological order.

Use full stops where needed to separate clauses.

1 The numbers have now stabilised at about 2000, nevertheless, the poaching threat remains great.

2 Fewer than 200 Sumatran rhinos survive in the wild, furthermore, there is no indication the situation is stabilising.

3 The black rhino is in fact grey and often assumes the colour of the soil in which it wallows.

4 Over 200 poachers have been killed since 1984, however, poachers have killed 1170 rhinos.

5 The black rhino has a pointed lip, in contrast, the white rhino has a square lip.

6 Endangered species must be protected, otherwise, we will lose these precious animals forever.

Word study

There are often many ways to express the same idea. Group the words below under the five word headings in the chart. (Note: The words in each group may not mean *exactly* the same or be used in *exactly* the some contexts.)

limit	main	magnificent	remarkable	sector	border	major	verge
primary	edge	environment	territory	stunning	locality	breed	type
leading	class	awe-inspiring	variety	zone	region	kind	
amazing	chief	predominant	principal	brink	impressive	perimeter	

spectacular	dominant	species	area	boundary

Evaluating other people's writing

What is wrong with the student's report on tigers below? Mark at least five things in the report that could be improved, e.g.

- content (e.g. relevant to task and type of text)
- report structure
- vocabulary and grammar
- punctuation

There are many types of tigers. Today only about 5000 wild tigers live across Asia. Asia is the only place that tigers live. This includes Russia where the Siberian tiger lives. Some tiger species have become extinct already and if we do not do something dramatic very soon, some others will soon be extinct too.

The Bengal tiger lives in India. Although some also range through Nepal, Bangladesh, Bhutan and Myanmar. There are about 3000 or 4000 Bengal tigers left, so as you can see they are the largest subspecies. There are about 300 in captivity (zoos).

The Bengal tiger is under threat of extinction like all tigers. The major reasons are poaching, habitat loss and population fragmentation.

Across Asia, vast forests have been taken for timber or converted to farmlands and this means that there is very little space for tigers. This means they cannot find food. Tigers are poached for their bones, whiskers and other body parts.

There are programs to help save the tiger so at least something is being done, but the situation is still serious.

Quick think

How much do you know about these endangered species? Underline the correct answer.

1 There are approximately ______________________ rhinos of any type left in the world.

a 25 000 **b** 2000 **c** 100 000

2 In 1982 there were 1.2 million wild African elephants. Now there are about ______________________.

a 1.5 million **b** 600000 **c** 2000

3 There are between ______________________ giant pandas left in the wild.

a 5000 and 8000 **b** 1000 and 2000 **c** 500 and 1000

4 It is estimated that there are fewer than 60 000 koalas left in Australia, but every year approximately ______________________ are killed by dogs and motor vehicles.

a 100 **b** 4000 **c** 400

Proofreading

Correct the spellings where necessary. Check your corrections against the chapter vocabulary list.

dominent	verge	extiction	predaters	bounderies
endangerment	crisis	catastrophic	proportions	venrable
drastic	spectaclar	poaching	ceremonal	daggers
intense	stabilation	sancturies	encourageing	magnifisent

Writing paragraphs and whole texts

1 Sequence this paragraph about the reasons for the endangerment of tigers. Use the words in italics to guide you. They provide links between the ideas in each sentence. Here is the first sentence to help you.

In the past, the main reason for the decline in the numbers of tigers and other big cats was that they were being hunted for their beautiful fur.

a *Now, however*, the situation is more complicated and there are *many factors* that threaten their existence.

b Even though it is illegal to kill a tiger, wild tigers *are being poached* for their bones, whiskers and other body parts.

c The *largest factor* is their loss of *habitat*.

d As *forest space* is reduced, the number of animals left is also reduced and tigers cannot find the prey they need to survive.

e Across all of Asia, once *vast forests have disappeared*—either cut down for timber or cleared for agriculture.

f *As a result*, tigers begin to eat the livestock of villagers and sometimes even attack humans.

g *Another threat* to the existence of tigers is *poaching*.

h *In turn*, the villagers sometimes kill the tigers to protect themselves and their livestock.

____

2 Use the notes below to write two to three short paragraphs about the Bengal tiger. Think carefully about how you will group the information into paragraphs.

Related species—7 other subspecies of tiger, e.g. Siberian tiger and Sumatran tiger—all endangered

Habitat—most found in eastern India and Bangladesh, also found northern and central India, Nepal and Myanmar—needs large home range—up to 100 square metres

Length—male up to 3.1 metres

Weight—male 180–260 kilos

Diet—deer, monkey, wild boar

Shoulder height—up to 0.9 metres

Number of young—2 to 4 occasionally more

Life span—15 years

Use the space below and opposite for your draft.

____

____

____

____

____

3 Choose an animal you know quite a lot about. It could be a domestic animal such as a dog or a cat, or it could be a wild animal. Think about what you would include in a factual report about this animal (e.g. definition, different categories or types, appearance, diet). Use your own paper.

a Write a plan for your report, listing the paragraph topics and making a few notes.

b Convert your plan into a short report (about 200 words).

CHAPTER 15

Poem

STRUCTURE

overall structure reflects text purpose—to express personal thoughts and feelings (in whatever way poet wishes to do so)

structure of poems varies widely—some have no definite structure (free-form) and others are very structured (e.g. certain number of rhythmic beats per line)

poem usually, but not always, broken up into verses

poetry generally meant to be read aloud, so sound of words important

Lockers

by Erica Fryberg

Crusts, crumbs and crumpled cardboard!
Soggy chips sag in spilt Coke trails,
Lollies melt on scurf-clogged haircombs
Caressed by waving cockroach feelers.
Other girls dump their books in rubbish
Shut the door and turn the key.

I treasure private places,
Personal hoards in hidden holes.
Sheltered dark, without tuckshop debris,
Blankets texts I don't need daily—
Entomb them in my tin-walled locker!
Close the door and turn the key.

Tests, deadlines, homework … pressure
Myriad threats oppress clear thoughts.
Why can't those be concealed in lockers?
Bury the abstract with the concrete:
Savagely shove both in a prison
Slam the door and turn the key.

I would lock up spiteful rumours.
Gossiping gangs and hostile glares,
Jealous feuds linked to competition,
Loneliness, bitter ostracism …
I'd hurl those burdens into darkness
Lock the door and lose the key.

LANGUAGE FEATURES

alliteration *(repetition of consonant sounds in words close together), e.g. 'crusts, crumbs and crumpled cardboard'*

language chosen that creates images in reader's mind, e.g. 'spilt Coke trails'

unusual use of words, e.g. 'caress' to describe what cockroaches do

freedom of use of language —use of words, grammar and sounds in ways not common in other writing

metaphor *(figure of speech in which one thing is said to be another), e.g. 'prison' to refer to the locker*

repetition of words links the ideas in poem—here the last line of each verse

Comprehension

Poems can be rather difficult to understand. This is because the writers are not so concerned with writing clearly to ensure the reader understands every single thing—as with factual texts.

Instead, they are concerned with expressing what they feel. In part, they are writing for themselves as much as for others. Usually, therefore, we have to work hard to relate the words on the page to emotions we have felt or experiences we have had.

1 Make a list of all the things you know about the writer from the words of the poem.

Often the words on the page mean more than, or even something different from, what they would mean in another everyday text and context.

2 The title of the poem 'Lockers' is simple and concrete, but the theme is complex and abstract. Underline which of the following you think best sums up the theme of the poem.

a friends and enemies at school

b the problems of adolescence

c the need for privacy at school

d taking care of possessions

3 From the way they are used in the poem, what do you think these words mean?

a scurf ______

b debris ______

c entomb ______

d ostracism ______

4 Answer these questions.

a In verse 1, why has the writer written the word 'other' in italics? ______

b In verse 2, what is it that 'blankets texts'? ______

c In verse 3, who do you think makes 'threats'? ______

d In verse 4, what does the writer mean by 'jealous feuds linked to competition'?

5 How would you describe the writer's feelings about her world at school on the basis of this poem?

6 What is your response to this poem? Are there particular lines or particular words that relate to your own experiences or feelings? Write two or three lines to express your personal response.

Writing skills

When writing poems you have quite a lot of **freedom** in the way you express your **ideas**, the **language** you use to do this, and the **structure** you choose. You can use traditional poetic techniques such as rhyme and alliteration, or not use them. Your choices will depend in part on your purpose and your theme.

1 The writer of the poem 'Lockers' does not use rhyme at the ends of lines, but she establishes a rhythm through her choice of words. Read the poem out loud to hear the rhythm.

2 The writer of the poem uses **alliteration**—that is, the repetition of consonant sounds in words close together, e.g. the repetition of 'cr' and 'c' in *crusts, crumbs and crumpled cardboard*. Underline all examples of alliteration you can find.

3 Why is it unusual to use the word *caress* in association with cockroaches? What effect does this have on you and on your image of the girls' lockers?

____

____

____

4 The writer uses the last line of each verse to give **cohesion** (unity) to the ideas in the poem. Read these lines again and look closely at the verbs she uses. What feelings does she express through these verbs, and what are the feelings about?

____

____

5 What vivid images are conveyed of the other girls' lockers (verse 1) and the girls themselves (verse 4). Circle the words in the poem that create these images.

____

Vocabulary

crumpled	**clogged**	**caressed**	**hoards**	**debris**
entomb	**myriad**	**threats**	**oppress**	**concealed**
abstract	**savagely**	**shove**	**spiteful**	**rumours**
hostile	**feuds**	**ostracism**	**hurl**	**burdens**

1 Underline the letters of the words that you find difficult to remember, e.g. the 's' in *debris*. Learn the words using the Look, Cover, Write, Check method.

2 Cover up the words above. Now test yourself by choosing which of the following word sets is correctly spelled.

a miriad, ostracism, hords, caressed, concealed

b myriad, ostracism, hoards, caresed, consealed

c myried, ostercism, hoards, caressed, concealed

d myriad, ostracism, hoards, caressed, concealed

e myriad, ostrecism, hoards, caressed, consealed

f myriad, ostracisem, hoards, carressed, concealed

3 Now choose the correctly spelled set of those below.

a entomb, savagely, feuds, shuve, threts

b entomb, savagely, feuds, shove, threats

c entomb, savagely, feuds, shouve, thretts

d entomb, savagedly, fudes, shove, threats

e entoom, savagely, feudes, shove, threats

Focus on punctuation

Punctuating poems

In poetry, punctuation, like other aspects of language, is used in unusual ways. Sometimes it is not even used at all. Poets use it to highlight particular ideas and to help readers follow the ideas.

Look at the use of full stops, commas, capitals and other punctuation in these two short poems.

Boy by Danielle van Coervorden
He looks from the shadows,
Not wanting to be seen.
He is dark and mysterious.
An Outcast.
He watches the children play.
He wants to join,
Despite their taunts and jokes.
Why can't he be like them?

Hummingbird by Nicole Gardiner
jewel-like
minimal
it flits among
the flowers
clothed in brilliant attire
majestic poise
strong
dainty wings
lift it beyond earthly confines
to dance on the golden gate

1 What effect does the heavy use of punctuation create in 'Boy'? How does it relate to the subject?

____

____

2 What effect does the lack of punctuation create in 'Hummingbird'? How does it relate to the subject?

____

____

Select a word

Choose words from the vocabulary list that mean the same as these words.

1 gently touched, stroked or kissed ______________

2 broken or torn pieces of something, rubbish ______________

3 old arguments causing bitterness ______________

4 preventing someone from being part of a group ______________

5 throw ______________

6 secret collections ______________

7 violently, fiercely ______________

8 a very large (uncountable) number of ______________

Grammar

Similes and metaphors

- **Similes** and **metaphors** are often used in poetry. They are examples of **figurative language**—language that does not have the **literal**, or real, meanings of the words. Instead it creates images or 'word pictures' in our minds.
- **Similes** are figures of speech in which one thing is said to be like another. They take two forms:
  as … as … e.g. *as deep as the ocean*
  like … e.g. *the mist is like a blanket*
- **Metaphors** are figures of speech in which one thing is said to be another, e.g. *his eyes were jewels*

- We use similes and metaphors in everyday life as well, e.g. *as quiet as a mouse* (simile); *she is a dark horse* (metaphor used when someone has done something completely surprising).
- Sometimes we use an **extended metaphor** where the metaphor is carried on beyond a line. In a way, in the poem 'Lockers', the concept of school lockers is an extended metaphor for a place in the mind where we can put the things that upset us.

1 Here are some everyday similes for common adjectives. Write another that is more imaginative.

a as dark as night — as dark as ______

b as soft as a baby's bottom — as soft as ______

c as strong as an ox — as strong as ______

d as light as a feather — as light as ______

e as cool as a cucumber — as cool as ______

2 What do you think the writers meant when they wrote these metaphors?

a My mind is a black hole. ______

b Sleep is a soft cocoon. ______

c My feet are my voice. ______

d The wind is a whip. ______

e My heart is shattered glass. ______

Word study

Everyday sayings and proverbs are often based on metaphors. What do these everyday metaphors mean?

1 I will eat my words. ______

2 I put my foot in it. ______

3 She drives me up the wall. ______

4 He is a wet blanket. ______

5 He is treading on thin ice. ______

6 Don't make waves. ______

7 Don't lose your head. ______

8 I would cut off my right arm for her. ______

9 She thinks she's the cat's whiskers. ______

10 It was a dog's breakfast. ______

Evaluating other people's writing

Look at this poem by the writer of 'Lockers'. It is very effective, but different in many ways from 'Lockers'. Identify at least five ways in which it is different or similar, e.g.

- the subject or theme of the poem
- structure of the poem
- simplicity or complexity of ideas
- use of simile and metaphor or other imagery
- use of alliteration or other techniques to create sound patterns or effects

The Snake by Erica Fryberg

Susurrus amongst the leaves
Suspense, suspicion ...
Snake sighted!
Slipping, sliding, smoothly gliding
Threading, sewing, weaving, flowing,
Stitching its progress stealthily—
Treacherous, sinuous
A supple, silken, sable cord
Traces its initial on the canvas of the concrete.
Shock
Spins a strangling coil around my mind.

Quick think

Here are some famous poems. Can you complete the last names of the poets who wrote them.

1	'Kubla Khan'	Samuel Taylor C ____________
2	'Death Be Not Proud'	John D ____________
3	'The Lady of Shalott'	Alfred Lord T ____________
4	'Hiawatha'	Henry Wadsworth L ____________
5	'Ozymandias'	Percy Bysshe S ____________
6	'The Tiger'	William B ____________
7	'Jabberwocky'	Lewis C ____________
8	'The Owl and the Pussycat'	Edward L ____________
9	'Pied Beauty'	Gerard Manley H ____________
10	'The Road Not Taken'	Robert F ____________
11	'Ode on a Grecian Urn'	John K ____________
12	'The Man from Snowy River'	A.B. ('Banjo') P ____________

Proofreading

Correct the spellings where necessary. Check your corrections against the chapter vocabulary list.

crumled	cloged	caresed	hoards	debrie
entom	miriad	threats	opress	consealed
abstract	savagly	shuve	spitful	rumors
hostile	feuds	ostrasism	herl	burdens

Writing paragraphs and whole texts

1 These students were asked to use a simile to describe themselves, and to create a short poem around it. Read their poems and then write a short poem about yourself using the same idea.

Tiger by Hannah McLean
Sometimes I am like a tiger.
Cunning.
Brave.
Outsmarting my enemies.
Capturing my prey with ease.

Ice by Sophie Holmes
Sometimes I am like ice.
Cold.
Hard.
Frozen with frustration!
Cracking under pressure.

Lightning by Crystalline Cayabyab
Sometimes I am like lightning
Bright.
Loud.
Filled with anger, hurt
Striking anyone who attracts me.

2 Read this student's poem.

Night by Jessie Garbellini
The night is like an approaching army, that closes in on you,
An army of stars
It swallows you up in its blackness.
The night weaves its pattern of stars with a giant needle.
A needle threading time.
It weaves the path to your destiny.
The night, heavy and damp, with its magical rain,
Waters your thoughts.
And makes them bloom like flowers of the night
Even the night with its splendours,
Cannot resist the urge of day.
The day that brings new life, so the night can carry on.

a Underline the similes and metaphors, and take note of the way the writer extends them over the lines.

b Make a list of other similes and metaphors you could use to describe the night.

c Extend your metaphors or similes into a poem like this one. Use the space opposite for your first draft.

3 In the space below, write a poem on a subject or theme of interest to you. You might want to write about:

- a part of the day
- an animal
- some aspect of school life
- an event
- a part of nature
- yourself and your feelings
- a person you know
- a scene

One way to get going is to find some books of poetry. Look at what subjects and themes others write about and at how they write about them. However, remember that there is no single way to write poetry.

ANSWER SECTION

CHAPTER 1: BASIC ESSAY

Comprehension

1 a
2 physical, social and personal benefits
3 sportsmanship, leadership and the importance of teamwork
4 c
5 a
6 Yes—*Like me, they play sport for one simple reason—it is good fun.*

Writing skills

1 *The most obvious advantages are physical, but there are also social and personal benefits.*
2 **a** Yes
3 *in the first place, for example, also, furthermore, also* (para. 2); *secondly, for example, also* (para. 3), *thirdly* (para. 4)
4 **a** *Not everybody likes sport but most people agree that participation in sporting activity benefits us in many ways.*
  b *It also fosters good breathing techniques.*
  c *Many people, for example, form strong and lasting friendships through participation in sport.*

Reasons for rewriting:

- Sentence **a** was too personal and informal (conversational).
- Sentence **b** was too general. Rewritten sentence is more specific and exact.
- Sentence **c** was too personal. In rewritten sentence writer generalises from personal experience.

5 continuation of notes:
  - reduces risk of heart disease and high blood pressure
  - maintains good body weight—important for prevention of other health problems
  - benefits us socially
    - friendships
    - important lessons, e.g. sportsmanship, leadership, importance of teamwork
  - helps us develop personally—mentally and emotionally
    - teaches us how to win and lose
    - provides opportunity to set goals—trying for personal best
  - these are only some benefits—most people don't think about benefits—play sport because it's fun

Focus on punctuation

Commas after these words:

1 **a** disease, injury
  b walking, jogging, swimming, skipping
  c objects
  d hockey, netball, soccer
2 b

Select a word

1 maintain	2 striving
3 aspects	4 obvious
5 fosters	6 consciously
7 capacity	8 prevention

Grammar

1 **a** (Stress) <u>can be</u> dangerous.
  b (Heart disease) <u>is</u> the most common cause of death.
  c (Children) <u>get</u> a lot of exercise naturally.
  d (Regular exercise) <u>relieves</u> stress.
2 **a** and **d** are not sentences. Could be changed as follows:
  a Breathe deeply.
  d He/she is a very fit person.
3 **a**–NS, **b**–S, **c**–S, **d**–S, **e**–NS, **f**–NS, **g**–NS, **h**–S

Word study

2 involvement
3 reduction
4 improvement
5 development
6 value
7 relaxation
8 protection
9 treatment
10 exercise

Evaluating other people's writing

Improvements that could be made include the following:

- Change introduction so that it clearly states the topic of the essay and indicates what areas will be covered; also omit detail about how sport helps us physically—this should be in a body paragraph.
- Make less personal throughout, e.g. omit *I like sport, my best friends, I have played, I know that I am stronger.*
- Combine some sentences to link ideas and make less 'choppy'.
- Omit direct, personal appeal to reader, i.e. *I think you should try it.*
- Reorganise paragraphs so that each one is about one area of sport only.

- Extend ideas more with examples—the essay covers some important and relevant ideas but does not organise them well or develop them far.

Quick think

1 true
2 true
3 false
4 true

Proofreading

These four sentences are incomplete. A possible way to change each is in brackets:

- Meaning beating your previous best effort. (This means beating your previous best effort.)
- The same in swimming. (It is the same in swimming.)
- Being a short way of saying 'personal best'. (This is a short way of saying 'personal best'.)
- Stopping many athletes from becoming downhearted about not always winning. (This stops many athletes from becoming downhearted about not always winning.)

Writing paragraphs and whole texts

1 e, b, a, d, c

2 A sample paragraph based on the notes could be:
Sport teaches the importance of teamwork. Team games such as football and netball do this most effectively, but so too do relay events in swimming and athletics. In sport we learn to trust our team-mates, and this is a very important lesson. We also come to understand that individuals have different strengths and weaknesses. Another valuable lesson we learn from sport is the importance of always doing our best because others depend on us. This experience teaches us to be responsible in other areas of our lives. Teamwork is perhaps the most important of all the social lessons we learn from sport.

4 A sample conclusion could be:
It is because of the great physical, social and personal benefits of sport, that there is such a strong emphasis on sport and physical activity in our society today. The points raised in the essay are a reminder that we probably should all be playing at least a little more sport than we do at present.

CHAPTER 2: DISCUSSION ESSAY

Comprehension

1 c

2 Single-sex education might be better for girls because boys can demand more of the teachers' time. Single-sex education may give students a better chance in subjects where one sex or the other traditionally does better.

3 Coeducation may prepare students better for the real world. Both boys and girls can have a good effect on the classroom in mixed classes.

4 Because girls sometimes think that boys do better in maths and science, they may not try to do well in these subjects if in mixed classes.

5 Mixed-sex schooling gives both boys and girls a chance to learn how to get on with each other and they need to be able to do this in the world of work.

6 b

Writing skills

1 *one important question their parents have to consider is whether it would be better to send them to a single-sex school or a mixed-sex (coeducational) school*

2 General. The writer just gives the broad ideas of the arguments to follow in the essay body, namely *educational* and *social*.

3 *These arguments may appear strong reasons to send a girl or boy to a single-sex school, but there are also reasons to favour mixed-sex schooling.* (See first sentence, para 4.)

4 c

5 para. 2—*One of the main arguments for segregated education is the fact that boys demand more of their teachers' time.* para. 3—*Another argument for separate schooling is that it gives students a better chance to do well in subjects where one sex or the other traditionally does better.* para. 4—*The strongest argument is that it prepares students better for the real world, especially the world of work where in general people have to work with both sexes.* para. 5—*Another argument in favour of coeducation is that both boys and girls can have a good effect on the classroom.*

6 All three original sentences were too personal and expressed in informal, everyday language, e.g. *I reckon, cool*
   a *Girls sometimes think it is not feminine to do well in maths and science.*
   b *Overall the social arguments for combined schooling outweigh the mostly educational arguments for segregated schooling.*
   c *Both males and females need to learn to get on with one another …*

7 Notes:
Is single-sex schooling better than mixed-sex schooling?
- single-sex schooling better
  - because boys demand more of teachers' time and this is not fair to girls
  - students may do better in subjects where traditionally boys or girls do better
- mixed-sex schooling
  - prepares students better for the real world, especially of work—males and females have to learn to get on with each other
  - boys and girls can have a good effect on the classroom
- overall, mixed-sex schooling better especially because of social learning

Focus on punctuation

Commas after:

1 **a** classes
   b schools
   c place
   d attention

2 d

Select a word

1 segregated
2 appropriately
3 favour
4 consider
5 outweigh
6 traditionally
7 system
8 appropriate

Grammar

1 a I think there are social benefits.
b Students can be distracted by the opposite sex.
c Academic achievement is an important issue.
d My local school is coeducational.

2 a Do you think students benefit educationally?
b Schools often offer single-sex classes.
c My sister happily attended a single-sex school for six years.
d Students sometimes have to travel long distances to find a single-sex school.

3 d

Word study

1	affect	2	effect
3	effect	4	affected
5	affecting	6	effects

Evaluating other people's writing

Improvements that could be made include the following:

- Change introduction so that it introduces topic and gives essay map of body paragraphs—this introduction goes straight into the detail of the argument.
- Overall make essay less personal—convert personal experiences (e.g. I have friends at the co-educational school in the next suburb ….) into general statements (e.g. *girls tend to think about their appearance when they go to school with boys*).
- Omit direct questions to the reader, e.g. *Do you remember primary school?*
- Change informal everyday language, e.g. *could not stand this, reckon, I suppose.*
- Avoid statements that cannot be supported with reasonable argument or fact, e.g. *girls are just so much better behaved I reckon.*
- Omit *as you can clearly see* in the conclusion—this is a dangerous statement, especially when the reader cannot clearly see what you have argued.

Quick think

1–c, **2**–d, **3**–f, **4**–b, **5**–a, **6**–e

Writing paragraphs and whole texts

1 **a**–ii, **b**–i, **c**–ii
2 e or a (most certain), b, c or d, f (least certain)
3 b, d, a, f, c, e

CHAPTER 3 PERSONAL RECOUNT

Comprehension

1

	Recount 1	Recount 2
When did the events take place?	Morning of 21 August	One morning last term
Where did they take place	Adventure World	St Stephen's Church graveyard
Why did they take place?	Design and technology excursion and asssigment	History excursion and assignment
Who was involved?	Year 9 design and technology class	Year 9 history class

2 a singing
b She was sick on the Pirate Ship ride.
c To be humorous—pretending that the class were serious about the assignment and focused on schoolwork (as the teachers wanted them to be), when in fact they were really thinking more about having fun because they were at Adventure World.

3 a Because they were going to a graveyard.
b Knowing what would happen if they did not do their work.
c Probably not. The first paragraph gives a few clues about the writer's attitude to ghosts. He mentions fear of hauntings and graves in the same breath as fear of not finishing the work. This gives the impression he is exaggerating his fear for humorous effect. It is the same in the last paragraph. He mentions the maths enthusiast's photo and then quickly moves to a light-hearted mention of the next history assignment.

Writing skills

1 The writers write in a general way about the events of the day; they leave out a lot of detail—they only include detail about interesting events.

2 **Recount 1**: … *morning on 21 August; En route; When we arrived; During the day*
Recount 2: *One morning last term; after being handed a worksheet; the next day; by the day after; This continued for around two weeks straight; By the second last visit; As the last day of the assignment dawned; when our photos were developed; just as everyone was enjoying a sense of relief that they had not been possessed*

3 **Recount 1:** *we were blessed with the voices of a host of angels … and one Daniel Everson; … were not allowed to enjoy ourselves; … and generally* not *have a good time; … there was an accident that involved Donna Squires, the Pirate Ship and an urgent need for a bucket; … (even though, as already mentioned, none of us had a good time).*
Recount 2: … *but we were more petrified by what we might face if we didn't finish our work; … (well, most of us did); … (there's no understanding some people); The same girl who did her maths homework had actually photographed a ghost!; … we were presented with the assignment sheets for the next historic outing!*

4 **a** uninteresting and unnecessary detail
b does not capture the humour of the situation
c and **d** Information seems irrelevant to the recount, but could be made relevant if linked with the events.

Focus on punctuation

Commas after:

1 month
2 surprise
3 nevertheless
4 hours
5 finally
6 trek

Select a word

1 urgent
2 destiny
3 faults
4 terrified
5 possessed
6 trekked
7 chill
8 blessed

Grammar

1 a The Year 9 Food Technology class cooked for the parents.
b Peer Support leaders welcomed the new students.
c The annual walkathon got off to a great start at 9 am.
d The end point of the trip was the Warragamba Dam.
e A hearty lunch kept us going for the rest of the afternoon.
f Ten students from Year 9 took part in the concert.
g Having lunch at McDonald's and then some nap-time in the bus were the highlights of the trip for some people.
h Climbing the hill to the lookout was definitely not the best way to end the long day.

2 **a**–NS, **b**–NS, **c**–NS, **d**–S, **e**–S

Word study

1, 2 and **3**
have a similar meaning—that is, it frightened or disturbed me very much. (Sometimes the speaker may mean these things literally—that is, the speaker's hairs did feel as though they were standing, the speaker actually got goosebumps, or the speaker's skin did feel as though it was moving; but speakers often use these expressions to show how frightened they were, even when they have not actually had the physical reactions.)

4 We worked very hard. (*Trojans* refers to people from the ancient city of Troy.)
5 We were in a difficult situation where we would fail completely (sink) if we did not take control and help ourselves (swim).
6 We showed people who might not expect it that we were strong.
7 We had not quite finished the task (or competition), but it was already clear that we would achieve it (or win it). ('Hosed' refers to horses being hosed or washed down after racing.)
8 The day began well (or badly).

Evaluating other people's writing

Improvements that could be made include the following:

- Include an orientation (title and first sentences) that tells clearly what events are being written about, when and where they happened, and who was involved.
- Omit boring details, e.g. about which carriages of the train people sat in.
- Omit comments about parts of the trip that were boring.
- Include more specific information instead of making general statements, e.g. *went pretty well.*
- Avoid repetition—*had a good day, had a pretty good day.*
- Include more interesting comment on events.

Quick think

	1 A								2 S	U	C	C	E	3 S	S			
	4 R	E	L	I	E	V	5 E	D						U				
	R						V							R				
	I						E							P				
	V						N							R		6 I		7 B
	E						T		8 E	X	P	E	R	I	E	N	C	E
	D		9 F				U							S		S		H
			I				10 A	S	S	11 I	G	N	M	E	N	T		A
12 C	A	R	N	I	V	A	L			N				D		R		V
			N				L			I						U		I
			A				Y			T						C		O
			L							I						T		U
			Y							A						I		R
					13 A	N	N	U	A	L						O		
										L						N		
				14 J	O	U	R	N	E	Y								

Writing paragraphs and whole texts

1 Here are the two recounts unjumbled:
On Monday, 21 September, our prayers were finally answered! The two Year 9 geography classes went on an excursion. We spent the day visiting the Sydney Aquarium, watching movies at the Imax, chasing ducks in knee-deep water and generally wreaking havoc on the whole of Sydney! One major disappointment was discovering the 3D movie was only 2D. We can't, however, overlook the *educational* aspect of the excursion as numerous (ahem) students filled out their worksheets. Congratulations to Ms Makis and Mr Maharaj, who managed to keep us under some sort of control and get us back alive and well!
Thursday, 30 April, was a day that stretched our calf muscles, our endurance and later our stomachs as, once again, PHS held its annual cross-country carnival. As usual, the day began early so that all races could be held before the now famous cross-country barbecue. The younger age groups ran first with some outstanding

successes from newcomers to the school, Sophie Bromfield and Matt Stanowski. Then it was the turn of the Under 15s with Tom Richardson (surprise, surprise) and Skye Blakeney breaking school records by several minutes. After a tough battle, Wentworth House finally won the day. The SRC barbecue proved to be a great success as usual, and was much appreciated by the runners, joggers (!) and spectators.

2 d, b, a, c, f, e, h, g
Paragraph 1: meanwhile, eventually
Paragraph 2: suddenly, eventually
Paragraph 3: at first, at last
Paragraph 4: in the end

CHAPTER 4: INSTRUCTIONS

Comprehension

1 a, c, f
2 **a** to allow one or two to go for help in an emergency
b for emergency signalling
c because if you do not, the victim's body might lose its ability to keep warm
3 **a** A kilometre will probably seem much further than that because of walking conditions.
b You should adapt how fast you go and how often you rest to suit all the members of the group—not just the fastest and fittest ones.
c Look at your map and compass often so that you know where you are going and how long it is taking you to cover the distance.
d Mountain areas are very likely to have sudden changes of weather.
4 at the end of Stage 2

Writing skills

1 **b** Stage 4: Air searches for lost persons; because, like most instructions, these instructions are organised in the time sequence they would occur and air searches would follow next after bushwalkers getting lost. Also, the last words of Stage 3 give a hint of what would follow.
2 recognise, remember, travel, give (details), give (serious thought), wear, take (a change of clothes), take (a safety kit), try to be aware, (don't) panic, sit, try to plan, mark, leave, do not walk, make, await. The purpose of instructions is to tell the reader what to do. This sentence pattern makes it easy for readers to see what they must do because the words that contain this information (the verbs) come early in the sentence.
3 No single correct answer. A possible answer is:
Don't panic!
Mark the route
Leave a dated note
Do not
Light a fire
4 **a** *Also take a safety kit which includes …* (original assumes too much about the reader; instructions are usually written for people who do not know much about the subject)
b *Always try to be aware of your rate of progress and direction of travel by …* (original does not give enough information—does not tell you how to be aware of where you are)
c *Don't panic!* (original not strong enough)
d *Do not walk at night or in sleet, snow or fog* (original is not a complete sentence and meaning is unclear—does not follow the typical pattern shown in exercise 2.

Vocabulary

1 approximately
2 definitely
3 essentially
4 personally
5 principally
6 considerably
7 incredibly
8 naturally
9 entirely
10 simply

Focus on punctuation

1 Check against original on page 24.
2 c

Select a word

1 hazard
2 periodically
3 regulated
4 prone
5 pace
6 proposition
7 visible
8 sheltered

Grammar

1 **a** travel (1 clause)
b give (1)
c Wear (1)
d Don't panic (1)
e make, light (2)
2 **a** It is important to have enough food when you go camping, but you need to think carefully about how much you can carry.
b Bring ingredients for a sandwich, and make them up when you stop for a rest.
c Marshmallows are fabulous to toast over a fire. Hot chocolate is a great tea or coffee substitute.
d Packets of soup are good for crisis times. They provide warmth and instant energy.
e You should not take too much food with you, but you don't have to starve and suffer.
3 b, d

Word study

1–d, **2**–j, **3**–a, **4**–i, **5**–g, **6**–h, **7**–f, **8**–e, **9**–c, **10**–b

Evaluating other people's writing

Improvements that could be made include the following:

- Add a heading or first sentence to show clearly the purpose of the instructions.
- Change sentences so that most follow the pattern shown in the sentence *Get out of the wind*, e.g. change *Staying close …* to *Stay close …*
- Fix sentences that are not complete, e.g. change *Also long underwear* to *You should wear long underwear.*
- Omit questions to the reader—you should tell them the information, not ask questions.
- Break up long sentences, e.g. sentence beginning *Huddling together …*
- Generally organise information into logical chunks and arrange in bullet points (•) or numbers to make it easier to follow.

Quick think

1 true
2 true
3 false
4 false
5 true
6 true
7 true
8 false

Proofreading

Conserving water is essential. Use creek water for washing up, but do not wash in the creek as food residue can harm the creatures that inhabit it. Think about what your water needs are. Do not drink too much water. Sip it at regular intervals rather than drinking it in large quantities at less frequent intervals. Your body will absorb it better. If you must use creek water, boil it or bring a couple of water-purifying tablets. They taste awful but will do the job.

Writing paragraphs and whole texts

1 **a** avoid
b use
c make
d indicate
e lay out
f provide
g make
h expose
i try

2 **a** If you've planned a long hike for the weekend but the forecast is for mid-30s temperatures, then go to the movies and do it next weekend.
b If there is a heavy storm, try to find shelter under a rock or in a cave.
c If there is lightning, avoid isolated trees and powerlines.
d If you are considering a hike in the remote wilderness, consider buying a short-wave radio or a satellite phone.
e If you see a snake, the safest thing to do is avoid it.

CHAPTER 5: BOOK REPORT

Comprehension

2 b, d, e, a, c **3 a** true **b** false **c** true d false **4** c

Writing skills

1 **a** para. 3, after sentence ending … *later on in their adventures*
b para. 4, after sentence ending … *in one day*
c para. 1, after sentence ending … *work out their options*
d para. 2, after sentence ending … *record what has happened*

2 **a**, **c**, and **d** are all possibilities. **b** is not very useful because it is about a place in the book and does not convey much about the exciting and frightening plot. The best quotation is perhaps **a** because it gives a sense of how exciting and dramatic the story is (and this is what the report focuses on). It is also suitable because we can understand what it is about without having read the book. **c** would also be suitable—it is actually the first lines of the book and shows how the story is in fact a diary, and this is referred to in the report. **d** is not quite as good as **a** and **c** because it does not clearly set a scene—that is, we do not know what moment is being described.

3 a, b
is, go, return, discover, is, retreat, work out, hide, try to do, fight, is told, (has been chosen,) record, illustrates, change, are described, is thinking about, is worrying, are, (is) working out
c para. 3 uses the present mainly but the past is used—*have grown, (have) learned*—to talk about the change in the characters from the beginning of the book to the end of the book (two different points in time); in the last paragraph, again the writer uses the present, but also uses the past—*found, read*—to talk about her own experiences with the book. She uses the past because she has finished reading the book.

4 *fantastic, terrifying, tense, exciting, frighteningly realistic, unputdownable*

5 It means you can't put the book down or away because you are so engrossed in the story.

Vocabulary

se-clud-ed, caul-dron, boul-ders, fer-al, in-vad-ed, cha-os, terr-i-fy-ing, out-rage-ous, res-cue, re-treat, op-tions, de-cide, ill-u-strates, in-no-cent, cour-age-ous, des-per-ate, ex-tra-ord-i-nary (in everyday speech, the second and third syllable are usually said as one syllable), tense, lit-er-al-ly, re-com-mend

Focus on punctuation

1 Quotations marks around
a 'The Hitch Hiker's Guide to the Galaxy'
b 'A Midsummer Night's Dream' **c** 'Tomorrow, When the War Began' 'I just hope we can survive',
d 'The Australian' **e** 'West Side Story'. (Note: Single or double quotation marks may be used.)

2 d

Select a word

1 literally
2 options
3 chaos
4 cauldron
5 feral
6 retreat
7 illustrates
8 secluded

Grammar

1 a When they get back their parents have been taken hostage.
   b The small group decide to go back to town, even though they are terrified.
   c The book only took me one day to read because I simply could not put it down.
   d You really want to read the next book as soon as you finish this one.
   e You should give this book a go, despite what you may have heard.
   f If you want non-stop action thrills, this is a brilliant choice.
2 Possible answers:
   a before
   b even
   c As soon as
   d until
   e when/whenever
   f unless
3 **a**—iii, **b**—v, **c**—iv, **d**—ii, **e**—i
   The only sentence in real need of a comma is **d** *This book is futuristic fantasy, whereas the author's last book was set in a real time and place.* You could also add a comma to **a** *The book will appeal to all ages, although it is written mainly for young adults.* The other sentences don't need one, as they are quite short and a comma is not needed for clarity.

Word study

authentic, believable, true-to-life, realistic, accurate; action-packed, lively, not a dull moment, adventure-filled; comic, hilarious, humorous, witty; suspenseful, tense, taut, mysterious; tragic, moving, heart-breaking; glued to, engrossing, hooked, gripped

Evaluating other people's writing

Improvements that could be made include the following:

- Add introduction (title and first sentences), which immediately identifies title, author and perhaps type of book.
- Break up into paragraphs that focus on plot summary, characters and opinion—at present all these parts are jumbled together.
- Give more detail about characters instead of simply saying *I liked all the characters.*
- Give more information overall so that readers can make sense of it, even if they have not read the book—this writer assumes that readers have read it.
- Use more interesting words than *good, like, great time.*
- Avoid overworked words such as *amazing.* (This writer has used *amazing* three times.)
- Give reasons for opinions—say why the book is *amazing*, why Marsden is *brilliant.*
- Omit informal, conversational language, e.g. *I guess, kids, this group of kids, best bits, my mum* and use more formal language instead.
- Fix incomplete sentence—change *Especially where they rescue Lee in the bulldozer* to *One of the most exciting parts is the incident where they rescue Lee in the bulldozer.*
- Break up *They go back to Hell first they have some amazing adventures* into two separate sentences or join with 'but'—*They go back to Hell but first they have some amazing adventures*.

Quick think

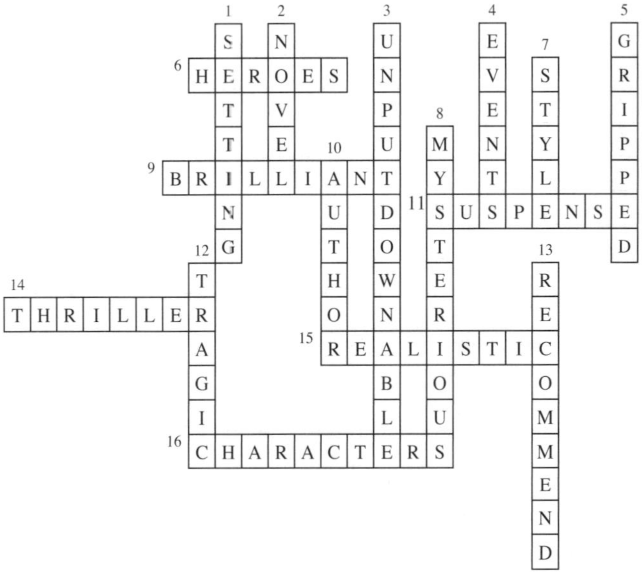

Proofreading

In *Z for Zachariah*, by Robert O'Brien, Ann Burden appears to be the lone survivor after a nuclear holocaust. She sees a column of smoke over the mountains coming closer each evening. In fright she moves to a cave and then watches another survivor come over the hill. It is a man by the name of Mr John Loomis. After recovering from a deadly illness, Mr Loomis seems to be threatening Ann's solitary life in the green valley. Ann must decide whether Mr Loomis is a friend or enemy. She must decide if the kind man she first knew has turned into a crazed maniac.

Writing paragraphs and whole texts

1 c, f, a, e, b, d
2 a I liked the characters because they were amusing and unusual.
   b The book was so thrilling that I convinced my parents to read it.
   c The book is a great read because it is action-packed as well as thought-provoking.
   d I did not like the book at all, because of the predictable characters and plot.

e This series has it all—action, suspense, romance and adventure.

Possible answers:

f I love this book because it is so realistic and moving.

g I thought it an excellent book with action, adventure and suspense on every page.

h He is my favourite character because of the way he develops during the story into a such a strong leader.

CHAPTER 6: DESCRIPTION OF A SCENE

Comprehension

1 a

d The main focus is on the people watching the game.

2 Any of the following words could help you decide that is a football game being described: *flies off into the sparkling sun, goalposts, player, two points, whistle blows, grandstand, match, beer and chips, offside, crashing over the line, scoreboard, full-time hooter, ball, uprights, number 12 swings his foot, ball sails high again and the flags are up, stadium*

3 a

4 b

5 He is surprised that people rarely fight physically when they are so passionate about the game and care so much about the results.

6 *All that matters is that you are yelling your lungs out*— the use of *you* instead of *they* suggests that the writer is part of the crowd himself.

Writing skills

1 *lies off, spinning, screeching, cheering, clapping, jeering, battles it out, leaps, waving, crashing, sprinting, zooms, leaping, scattering, whisks, thunder, waves, sails, grabs*

2 a crashing b sprinting c zooms d burn e whisks f thunder

3 Visual and sound images are used most. Visual, e.g. *flies off into the sparkling sun, spinning towards the goalposts, an old lady leaps from her wheelchair, waving her blanket in the air, a group of boys come sprinting past her, leaping over fans, scattering bags, chip cartons and other debris, baby girl under the layers of jersey …*; sound, e.g. *'GIIIRD-LAA, GIIIRD-LAA, GIIIRD-LAA, GIIIRD-LAA'. 'Whumpf.', all screeching fanatics—all on their feet cheering and clapping; All that matters is that you are yelling your lungs out: 'Are yer blind or sumthin?'… , The stadium is ringing with his name …* ; smell (and taste), e.g. *the smell of beer and chips overwhelms*; touch, e.g. *goes crashing over the line, desperate to touch the ball, Oh, to touch that ball*

4 a the ball (the ball is not referred to in the text—the writer is assuming we can work it out from the context)

b the *pimply teenagers, weather-beaten old men, women, kids—all screeching fanatics*

c *match of wit and passion*

d the *old lady*

e the *group of boys*

f the player called Girdler

5 para 2: the crowd watching the game

para 3: the crowd on the hill area of the stadium

para 4: a particular person in the crowd—an old lady in a wheelchair

para 5: a group of young boys as they follow the ball

para 6: a father and baby girl as they watch the game

In the final paragraph the writer returns to the focus of the first paragraph—the player, Girdler, having another attempt at a goal and this time being successful.

6 a *An old lady leaps from her wheelchair, waving her blanket in the air as her favourite player goes crashing over the line* (original sentence contains too many ideas and is confusing)

b *Oh, to touch that ball* (original has too many words and does not create the vivid image that the sentence in the final text does)

c *Pimply teenagers, weather-beaten old men, women, kids—all screeching fanatics* (original too general—does not create a vivid image of the people)

d *This time the hecklers don't get to him and he grabs back the two points he lost to them earlier* (original was in the past tense and was not consistent with the use of the present in the rest of the text—present tense makes the action seem closer)

e no sentence about the score in final version—information is not relevant to the description of the scene

Focus on punctuation

1 and 2

para. 1—it's (apostrophe of omission), they're (omission), they've (omission); para. 2—it's (omission); para. 3—where'd (omission—meaning 'where did'); para 4—she's (omission), there's (omission);
para. 6—it's (omission); para. 7—don't (omission)

3 a it's b its c its d it's

4 a

Select a word

1 debris
2 barely
3 overwhelms
4 meek
5 desperate
6 jeering
7 ritual
8 hecklers

Grammar

1 a Thousands fill the stadium <u>every weekend</u>.

b They play <u>like madmen</u> <u>for a full eighty minutes</u>.

c When the hooter went, a little old man <u>near me</u> cried.

d Mud spatters <u>onto the closest spectators</u>.

e The crowd rose <u>to their feet</u> <u>as one</u>.

2 Possible answers:

a Kids run onto the field, as the full time hooter sounds.

b Silence falls over the crowd, as he takes the kick.

c The ball flies over the tips of the goalposts.

d The noise in the grandstand gradually increases.

Word study

2 **a** win easily
b beat the opposition easily
c the team suddenly could do nothing right and began to lose
d the cheers were extremely loud (so loud they could have lifted the roof off the stadium)
e he always wants to win and does not take losing very well
f go from a losing position to a winning position at a certain point
g the stadium was absolutely filled—no space at all
h the crowd went wild in response to some incident
i,j play with every bit of your energy and enthusiasm
k win all or most games in the competition up till the present

Evaluating other people's writing

Improvements that could be made include the following:

- Add an opening to catch the reader's attention—this opening is very uninteresting.
- Add some interesting detail about the groups of people mentioned instead of just making general statements about them.
- Break up *I know I would, many of them are schoolchildren* into two sentences.
- Vary the length of the sentences—these are mostly very short sentences, which give the text a 'choppy' effect.
- Use some interesting action verbs to make the scene come alive.

Quick think

X	A	R	H	O	O	T	E	E	F	O	N	U	S
F	T	R	O	O	P	T	H	X	Y	P	T	E	I
E	A	K	W	A	I	L	R	J	E	E	R	Z	G
C	A	N	L	T	E	R	R	E	Z	O	U	N	H
H	L	E	M	R	O	S	C	A	N	R	S	E	A
E	D	E	S	P	S	H	O	U	T	H	O	C	R
E	A	B	C	A	N	D	O	H	O	M	E	A	A
R	V	A	L	B	A	R	R	A	C	K	U	A	R
B	A	R	L	Y	K	E	A	M	Z	M	A	N	Y
C	O	M	S	C	R	E	E	C	H	E	S	T	O
B	H	E	H	S	E	L	B	E	S	O	N	T	O
O	L	E	R	D	A	R	N	O	M	O	A	N	F
O	P	S	I	F	A	H	O	L	L	E	R	D	S
D	R	E	E	S	S	S	T	O	N	D	E	N	Q
F	G	R	K	A	G	E	T	Y	O	W	L	N	U
C	H	R	E	C	K	O	T	J	E	L	M	O	E
O	N	E	O	Z	O	M	E	D	R	L	E	A	A
R	Y	L	O	A	O	K	S	M	I	G	L	H	L
H	I	S	S	T	N	L	A	S	P	A	P	E	R

Writing paragraphs and whole texts

1 **a** Grey faces.
b Two down and two to go.
c Bit chilly this morning.
d Silence shattered.
e Lollies, crisps, even hot chips.
f Good news or bad news?

CHAPTER 7: SHORT STORY

Comprehension

1 and **2** loneliness (e.g. *his lone, faithful companions*), nature (e.g. *how foolish to think that man could conquer nature*), self-knowledge *(It was in that moment that he knew. He reflected upon his folly … to conquer nature*), relationships (relationship with father—*But he had something to prove … he had gone where his father had never been;* relationship with dogs—*his lone, faithful companions, freeing his dogs from their harnesses so they could escape*), death (*the land of death; He knew that if he was to fall into that water, he would die*). The most important theme is either self-knowledge or relationships.

3 a

4 **a** at the end of para. 3
b after first sentence, para. 4
c after first sentence, para. 5

5 **a** true
b false
c true
d false

6 the physical journey to Antarctica and the personal, emotional journey of self-discovery and self-knowledge

Writing skills

1 a, c, e

2 examples of descriptive language—*stumbling, blistering, tearing, fearless, shivered, plodded, doggedly, sharp eyes hunting, relentless, doomed, groaned, frigidity, meagre, lone, faithful, trudged, endless glare, panic, terror, howled*

3 d, i, f, h, c, b, e, a, j, g

4 The ending is resolved in the case of the man—we know he died, but it is not resolved in the case of the dogs—we do not know what happens to them. It is not necessary in a short story to complete all details of what happened at the end. It is usually more dramatic to leave something up to the reader's imagination.

Vocabulary

1 **a** thinned, thinning
b snapped, snapping
c wrapped, wrapping
d planned, planning
e stepped, stepping

3 b

Focus on punctuation

1 **a** no man's land
b his father's adventures
c the two dogs' harnesses
d the two young explorers' route
e the tent's opening

f the women's expedition
g the sun's glare
h the man's loneliness
2 a, c, e

Select a word
1 frigidity
2 wanting
3 unison
4 folly
5 oblivion
6 doggedly
7 relentless
8 reflected

Grammar
1 a He fell, crying out with pain.
b The ice closed in, trapping him without mercy.
c The sun beat down steadily, burning into his reddened flesh.
d Keeping himself quite still, he listened for other human sounds.
e The other expedition members, believing he had been killed, finally abandoned the campsite.
2 Possible corrections:
a As he was running along, a rock fell on his head, or Running along, he was hit by a falling rock.
b Crawling into the base camp, he saw the lights shining.
c Believing his time had come, he watched the polar bear approach.

Word study
Examples only:
1 the cold: arctic, biting, bitter, crisp, cutting, numbing, raw, piercing
2 the heat: baking, blistering, boiling, burning, fiery, searing, scorching, steamy, stifling, sweltering
3 the night: black, coal-black, gloomy, pitch-dark, inky, moonless, starless, shadowy
4 the desert: parched, arid, barren, scorched, stark, featureless, monotonous, flat
5 the city: vibrant, lively, hectic, crowded, cramped, congested, bustling

Evaluating other people's writing
Similarities include the following:
- Opening words immediately set the scene and introduce the main character in an interesting way.
- The subject of the story is a person and the focus is what is going on in his mind.
- Descriptive language is used effectively—writer does not overload with highly descriptive words but chooses them carefully and with good effect.
- Sentences vary in length including some very short ones.

Differences include the following:
- Main character is given a name.
- The setting is the city.
- There is more focus on the appearance of the main character.
- There is less focus on actions of the character.

Quick think
1 slither
2 shuffle
3 plod
4 stagger
5 stroll
6 limp

Proofreading
Frank slithered backwards and collapsed on the kerb. It felt gritty and hard. A cold wind picked up and blew past a copy of yesterday's news. Then all was quiet once again. Picking himself up unsteadily, Frank scratched his brow, then looked up and saw it was a cloudy, starless sky.

In the distance a payphone emitted a soulless fluorescent light. Frank's weary feet shuffled and slowly began to drag his battered old body towards it.

Writing paragraphs and whole texts
1 a fumbled
b fell
c clinging
d meshed
e pushing
f clanged
g stumbled
h dangled
2 g, b, e, a, c, f, d

CHAPTER 8: NEWS ARTICLE

Comprehension
1 c In paragraph 1 (*would-be thief, left with … an empty feeling*) and paragraph 3 (*fled empty-handed*)
2 b In paragraph 1 (*a phantom benefactor*), paragraph 2 (*quite intriguing … total mystery*) and paragraph 3 (*'That would destroy the mystery. It's better not to know'*)
3 a false b true
c false d false
4 a true b false
c false d true
5 a the counter assistant
b the intruder/would-be thief
c the person or persons who are putting flowers in the hands of the statue
d the type of flower

Writing skills
1 e, c, d, a, b
2 Writers use short paragraphs because people are more likely to read something if it looks easy to read and short paragraphs help give this impression. Also, because the writing is in columns, one sentence can often take up four or five lines.
3 In 'Try to buy…' it might be good to use the words of the McDonald's counter server, the manager and perhaps a customer if one saw the incident. Example of what counter server might say: 'The thief didn't look too sure about what he was doing so I thought I might have a chance of putting him off if I asked him to buy something.' The manager might say: 'I was very impressed at his initiative and bravery. It was very clever for someone so young to think of saying that.'

4 the headline *Try to buy before you steal; left with nothing more than an empty feeling; eager to oblige; but the frustrated intruder apparently changed his mind and fled empty-handed*

Vocabulary

1 experienced 2 eccentric 3 mystery
4 all correct 5 accommodate

Focus on punctuation

1 **a** 'We are asking everyone to take care in the area,' the spokesman said.
b 'Most people don't realise how demanding writing is,' said the famous author. 'They think you sit down and the words just flow out.'
c 'We hold grave fears for his safety,' said the sergeant in charge. 'The situation is very grim.'
d 'I've been through hell,' the young surfer said after being chased by a 2-metre shark.
e The zoo worker said, 'I was simply doing my daily job, feeding the bears when she suddenly turned on me.'
f 'His memory is not good and we are worried that he might have gone off somewhere,' the old man's daughter said tearfully.

(Note: Single or double quotation marks may be used.)

2 b

Select a word

1 confrontation
2 analogy
3 parallels
4 benefactor
5 eccentric
6 oblige
7 accommodate
8 Caucasian

Grammar

2 **a** Police last night were searching rugged bushland for a teenage boy who had gone missing after a furious row with his parents.
b The man who discovered the hidden money, was/had been bushwalking with friends.
c The fighting has been going on for two weeks now.
d A sick young Melbourne girl has discovered that she is about to receive one million dollars from a mystery benefactor.
e A neighbour last saw him in the front garden on Friday, but before that she had seen him many times walking around the area, and he had seemed fine.

Word study

a DEAL	**b** PLEA	**c** KEY
d CUT	**e** HIT	**f** DRIVE
g CLASH	**h** AXE	**i** BLAZE
j BAN	**k** BOOST	**l** SWOOP

Evaluating other people's writing

Improvements that could be made include the following:

- Change headline to make it more interesting and specific, e.g. include mention of spider, or funnel-web.
- Keep tense consistently in past tense forms—change *He cries out in pain and his friends go over to get his mother from her home. By this time Tim is unconscious* to *He cried out … friends went over … was unconscious.*
- Choose interesting detail to place at beginning of story or begin story with information that boy is now safe and then go back to beginning of story.
- Use more interesting language to describe what happened, e.g. replace *taken to hospital* with *rushed to hospital.*
- Include more interesting details instead of just saying what happened.
- Perhaps include the exact words his parents or the other children said.

Quick think

1–d, **2**–b, **3**–c, **4**–a

Writing paragraphs and whole texts

1 **a** survived
b said
c was heading/headed
d managed
e drank
f decided
g set off
h described
i made
j was driving
k thanked
l had thrown
m was recovering

2 Paragraph breaks could possibly go after *Cairns* (line 2); *two nights* (line 5); *shark* (line 8); *at the time* (line 11). However, there are other possibilities and you could have more breaks.

CHAPTER 9: SHORT OPINION TEXTS—BLOGPOSTS AND LETTERS TO THE EDITOR

Comprehension

1 **a** 3 **b** 1 **c** 2 **d** 4

2 **c** The letters may also aim to do a and b but neither are the main purpose of the two letters.

3 The writer compares how long the students will feel hungry and in discomfort and pain compared to the suffering of the children who actually live in hunger.

4 D

5

Competition between students about how much they raise	Text 2 (blogpost)
Publicity about celebrities taking part	Text 3 (letter)

Writing skills

1	Text 1	Text 2	Text 3	Text 4
Direct appeal to the reader	×	×		
Direct appeal to the editor			×	×
Factual evidence	×	×	×	×
Logical argument	×	×	×	×
Emotional language	×			
Comparison/Contrast	×			
Personal experience	×	×		×

2 **a** brilliant (1) awesome (2) ugly (2)
b Text 1

3 **a** I believe the media focus on them is too great (text 1, line 5)
b understand the power they have to encourage others to do likewise (text 1, line 4)
c What wasn't obvious from your coverage was that many schools across Australia organise their own events

4 A calm and reasonable tone is more likely to make you think that the writer is sensible and has thought out the arguments thoroughly. A calm and reasonable letter is more likely to make you agree with the point of view expressed than an emotional, sarcastic or insulting one.

5 *in comparison to; it was not as big as or eye-catching as; a more descriptive article*

Vocabulary

1 ex-cept, ex-act-ly, com-mit-tee, com-pet-ing, be-hav-i-our, vul-ner-ab-le, con-trib-u-tions, cel-eb-rit-ies, suc-cess, iss-ues, praise, en-cour-age, ac-know-ledg-ement, part-i-cu-lar, cov-er-age, bal-ance, com-plete-ly, gen-er-os-it-y, en-du-rance, chall-eng-es

2 **a** celebrities, challenge
b acknowledgement, contributions
c encouraged, participate
d generosity
e praise, endurance
f coverage, issues

Focus on punctuation

2 **a** Shepparton News, Sunrise Show
b *Neighbours*, 40 Hour Challenge
c Uluru, Alice Springs, Northern Territory
d ABC, *Heartbreak High*, 40 Hour Famine
e Summerdale High, Summerdale Stadium
f *To Kill a Mockingbird*, *Go Set a Watchman*

Select a word

1 acknowledgement
2 coverage
3 vulnerable
4 endurance
5 generosity
6 challenge
7 balance
8 issues

Grammar

1–e, **2**–c, **3**–b, **4**–a, **5**–d

2 **a** The class voted for the charity that they wished to support for the year.
b They awarded a prize to the boys whose project raised the most money.
c Everyone attended the auction which was expected to raise $10 000.
d The students who did the walkathon raised $3000 for the local charity.
e The event that we were all looking forward to so much was cancelled at the last minute.

3 **a** DC
b S
c DC
d DC
e S
f D
g S
h D

Word study

1 sickening (1), distressing (2), troubling (3)
2 insulted (1), offended (2), unsettled (3)
3 regretful (3), embarrassed (2), mortified (1)
4 foolish (1), ridiculous (2), unwise (3)

Evaluating other people's writing

Improvements that could be made include the following:

- Add an introduction which clearly identifies the topic and purpose of the letter—purpose especially is not clear in this letter.
- Break up letter into paragraphs.
- Omit unimportant details, e.g. *I wondered what could be the matter …*
- Fix incomplete sentence, e.g. change *Attempting to explain this to the young guard* to *He was attempting to explain this to the young guard*; change *Especially after reading last week …* to *This is especially important considering the story in your paper last week about racism …*
- Add a strong conclusion to reinforce purpose of letter.

Quick think

D	A	P	P	X	T	S	R	C	O	N	C	E	R	N	E	D	D	D
E	A	X	O	R	P	R	A	S	E	U	O	G	E	F	S	R	E	I
L	P	S	A	D	D	E	N	E	D	E	T	G	E	F	H	O	X	S
I	P	O	H	M	M	O	P	A	B	C	O	R	F	O	O	G	I	T
G	A	O	Z	A	N	X	I	O	U	S	Z	M	A	N	C	N	A	U
H	L	N	Y	O	M	F	E	E	M	D	M	O	Z	G	K	A	H	R
T	L	F	X	R	G	E	E	U	N	S	E	T	T	L	E	D	R	B
E	E	G	R	Z	O	P	D	I	S	G	U	S	T	E	D	D	O	E
D	D	I	S	T	R	E	S	S	E	D	T	R	O	U	B	L	E	D
X	E	N	C	O	U	R	A	G	E	D	O	O	C	K	D	E	L	L

Proofreading

I was horrified recently to hear that a young woman, convicted of tripping up an old man and stealing his money, was given a two year good behaviour bond. The old man was hospitalised for two months from injuries he received. Where is the justice in our society? Why aren't people put in jail for violent crimes like this? If they are not, then they will think that these are not serious crimes and commit them again very soon. I believe it is time to review our sentencing practices.

Writing paragraphs and whole texts

1 c

a gives evidence about the ugliness of the competition at the school last year, which is good and could be developed into a good point. However, there is no clear link to the previous posts and other posts on other topics may have come before this one, making its purpose unclear.

b links well to the previous posts on the subject but is very general, only mentioning 'good ideas'. Again this could develop into a good post with specific ideas.

c is the best beginning. It refers appropriately to the previous posts on the subject. It sets up the expectation that both helping the children and class competition will be mentioned. The word 'However' indicates further development of these ideas.

d gives a relevant viewpoint and again may develop well. The language is informal but appropriate for a student blogpost. Like **a**, however, there is no clear link to the previous posts so its meaning may not be clear to the reader if other posts have come between it and the previous ones.

e refers appropriately to the previous posts on the subject but only states the general topic. It gives no suggestion of what will be focused on in the post. Again, however, the writer might go on to write a meaningful post.

2 e, b, a, d, c

CHAPTER 10: BIOGRAPHY

Comprehension

1 a

2 **a** para. 3
b para. 6
c para. 2
d para. 4
e para. 7
f para. 5

3 **a** The arrest of Rosa Parks for refusing to move for a white woman.
b He led a bus boycott.
c It led to a change in the law about segregated seating on buses.
d Washington.
e His approach was non-violent.

4 Timeline should include this information

1929 Born Atlanta Georgia
1955 Rosa Parks arrested—King takes role of leader
late 50s, early 60s Rallies, sit-ins to campaign against racial injustice
1963 Washington rally ('I have a dream' speech)—*Time* Man of the Year
1964 Received Nobel Peace Prize
1968 Assassinated by James Earl Ray

Writing skills

1 *was, was shot* (para. 1), *was born, was, made* (para. 2), *became, spoke, happened, led, called, refused, was arrested, became* (para. 3), *was, led, went on, included, were, was, marched* (para. 4), *became, spoke, listened, have, stir, have, will rise, live, hold, are created* (para. 5), *was, had, was named, received* (para. 6), *was, was shot* (para. 7), *rocked, mourned, devoted, had* (para. 8). Some verbs in para. 5 are in present, *have*, because talking about today, and *have, will rise, live, hold, are created* because writer is quoting King's exact words.

2 *in 1929, at that time, in 1955, from that moment onwards, on 25 August 1963, in 1963, in 1964, in 1968, on April 4*

3 Para 1: in the United States of America
Para 2: in Atlanta, Georgia; in the deep south of the USA; in most southern states at that time
Para 3: in his church; in Montgomery, Alabama; on a bus; across the nation
Para 4: in Montgomery; at segregated lunch counters, demonstrations etc; to places where there were particular racial problems; through Washington, DC
Para 5: at the Washington rally
Para 7: in Memphis, Tennessee

4 Attitude to King is shown by words *tragically* (para. 1), *words still have the power to stir our hearts and minds* (para. 5), *brilliant, courageous, devoted his life to his people and his country, power to move an audience like no other* (para. 8).

5 **a** Personal opinion such as this not relevant in biography—focus should be on the facts with any opinion clearly linked to facts.
b This is not relevant—focus on King only.
c This is too much a personal expression of emotion—better to keep to how the world reacted to King's death, not how it makes the writer feel—again, because focus is on facts.

Vocabulary

1 Nouns: racism, segregation, injustice, oratory, creed, assassination, boycott, campaign, rally (last three words can be verbs but are nouns in text)
Verbs: arrested, stir, mourned, received
Adjectives: civil, racial, self-evident, brilliant, courageous
Adverbs: tragically, successfully

Select a word

1 boycott
2 rally
3 oratory
4 stir
5 creed
6 segregation
7 assassination
8 civil

Grammar

1 **a** line drawn from that to *1929*
b line drawn from This to *campaign for freedom*
c line drawn from this to *non-violent approach*
d line drawn from There to *Memphis*

2 Eddie Mabo was born in 1936 on Mer (Murray) Island in the Torres Strait. The government of Queensland controlled the island through its Island Council and because of a prank during his teenage years, he was exiled to the mainland. His sense of land was reinforced by this experience and by his learning during this time. In the sixties and seventies he worked as a gardener at James Cook University. He used this time to attend lectures and read books. It was there that he learned that his people did not own the island they had lived on for centuries.

Subsequently, in 1981, Eddie made a speech about land ownership. This sparked off a historic series of events to challenge the notion of 'terra nullius'—no man's land—which had been the basis of possession by the British in 1788. The first court battle was lost and, sadly, Eddie died of cancer in 1992, not knowing that only months later the court's decision was overturned and 'native title' was legitimised. Eddie's name is immortalised in the name of the decision and for his bravery, intelligence and passion for his people and his land.

Word study

1 feminist, feminism, femininity
2 socialist, socialism
3 nationalist, nationalism, nationality
4 disappointment
5 consumerism
6 economist, economical
7 performance
8 preference
9 sincerity
10 interviewee
11 breakage
12 approval
13 wastage

Evaluating other people's writing

Improvements that could be made include the following:

- Fix introduction so that it only explains who Albert Einstein is and why we remember him and take out information about birth and childhood.
- Reorganise all paragraphs so that they are only about one aspect of his life.
- Omit mention of how complicated the theory was—not relevant.
- Fix incomplete sentences, i.e. change *Teaching at the University of Zurich* to *He taught at the University of Zurich.*
- Express ideas in more formal and sophisticated language, e.g. change *was good at* to *excelled at.*
- Rewrite part about his movements from country to country—it is confusing as it is.

Quick think

1–j, **2**–i, **3**–h, **4**–d, **5**–g, **6**–c, **7**–e, **8**–a, **9**–f, **10**–b

Proofreading

Charles Dickens was born in Portsmouth on 7 February 1812. He grew up in great poverty. When he was 12 years of age, he was sent to work in a boot-blacking factory on the banks of the River Thames in London. His miserable time there, although brief, was to remain in his memory all his life. He continued to work there when his father was sent to prison because of his debts. It was customary, in those days, for whole families to go to prison with their fathers, and this is what happened in Charles' father's case. It was a very low and lonely point in young Charles' life.

Writing paragraphs and whole texts

1 **a** 11 years later
b at the age of only 13
c in 1906
d on the second voyage
e on 17 January 1912
f a month earlier
g On the return journey
h a year later

CHAPTER 11: SPEECH

Comprehension

1 c
2 She is speaking against capital punishment.
(The opening sentence and *Should we reintroduce it or not? I think not.*)
3 a, c, d, g, i
4 **a** If person A does wrong to person B, it is acceptable for person B to do something wrong to person A—in other words, take revenge.
b Making mistakes is part of being a human being; forgiving those who make mistakes is difficult and takes real goodness (god-like behaviour)
5 two reasons—because life imprisonment takes the criminal off the streets and that is all we need to do to keep the community safe, and also imprisonment is enough punishment for any criminal
6 b

Writing skills

1 a, b, e (If we kill the killer, we too deserve to be killed)
2 **a** *So, should we reintroduce it or not? What does it say to them about dealing with conflict and hardship? A good message would you say? Even if there is no doubt that someone has murdered should the state stoop to that level and murder as well? Is it fair to hold these people fully accountable for their wrongdoing? Is not society at least partly to blame?*
b This question could go at the very end of the speech. It is your opinion whether or not this improves the speech. The final words of the speech are strong, so it is not really needed. However, finishing with this question would definitely send the audience away thinking about the answer and the issue.
3 Possible places for pauses: definitely between each paragraph and after each question to the audience; after the first sentence; after each short, sharp group of words, e.g. *Capital punishment, A quick fix;* after the sentences *Think for a moment what sort of example this sets for the community at large, Killing will not stop crime, Caring will.*

Select a word

1	err	2	abolished
3	trauma	4	stoop
5	host	6	vicious, barbaric
7	deterrent	8	accountable

Grammar

1 b   2 b   3 a   4 a

Word study

illegal–legal; introduce–abolish; acquit–convict; guilty–innocent; imprison–release; poverty–wealth; abundance–lack; prohibited–permitted

Evaluating other people's writing

Improvements that could be made include the following:

- Add an introduction that catches the audience's attention and that clearly introduces the topic and purpose of speech.
- Reorganise speech so that it is clear which points are for and which are against capital punishment, e.g. put all points 'for' first and all points 'against' second.
- Also reorganise so that each section/paragraph is about one argument only—these points are very muddled together.
- Add details or statistics where needed, e.g. say how many countries have the death penalty and give examples; say how many US states have the death penalty and give examples.
- Make ending more interesting—e.g. add a question, an interesting comment, a quotation.

Quick think

Incorrect tips: make eye contact with only one person in the audience; always be serious; try to memorise your whole speech.

CHAPTER 12: ADVERTISEMENT

Comprehension

1 c

2 a

3 a young female musicians
  b young people (12–24) interested in arts or performance arts

4 e The words *You will be tutored in different aspects of the music industry* suggest that the advertisement is mainly targeting young people who have left school and are now ready to work, or those thinking about a career after leaving school.

5 a opportunity to form a band; opportunity to perform for the community; CD of your music; program is free; lunch is provided
  b free workshop, materials provided; food (munchies) provided

Writing skills

1 similarities: use of visuals to attract reader; heading that highlights main aspect of what is being advertised; contact details at end

2 differences: advertisement **A** uses questions to attract the reader whereas advertisement **B** just describes the workshops; advertisement **A** spaces out information more than advertisement B; advertisement **A** uses different print sizes to highlight information, whereas advertisement **B** uses the same print for all information except heading and phone number; advertisement **A** uses *we* and *you*, which makes it quite personal, whereas advertisement **B** does not and keeps the focus on the information

3 You could argue that advertisement **A** would be more effective than advertisement **B** because of use of layout, questions and personal language. However, both advertisements appear to be very effective for what they are advertising and for the amount of information that needs to be included. If advertisement **B** had to include more information, the layout would perhaps not be so effective. As it is, however, the visual in advertisement **B** is very eye-catching and this, plus the heading, would effectively attract readers

4 Sample questions: Interested in costume, design, sculpture, mask or techno-party wear? Or interested in the performance arts in general? Like to take part in an exciting (and free!) series of workshops in wearable body art?

5
- opportunity to form a band/group
- chance to perform for the community
- your own compilation CD to keep

6 Differences include: only key information words in this advertisement—no extended text (e.g. full sentences); no questions to engage audience; much less information—you would have to phone up for information about who they are interested in getting to audition, e.g. Do they want only experienced actors? Do they want particular ages?; more use of different print and layout effects, e.g. black and white blocks.

Focus on punctuation

Possible punctuation and layout:

Bored?
Feel like some interesting holiday action?
Ever tried snorkelling?

EXPLORE THE FASCINATING WORLD UNDER THE SEA

YOU'LL LOVE IT!

- individuals, small groups or large groups
- safe for kids
- two-hour, half-day, or whole-day trips
- $15 an hour
- concessions available

We provide wetsuits and all other gear you need

Ring Jai or Anika—(02) 6899 9999—NOW!!!!

Select a word

1 material
2 aspects
3 hosted
4 essential
5 munchies
6 tutored
7 compilation
8 wearable

Grammar

1 **a** Lessons are of half-hour or one-hour duration.
b Afternoon teas are available from 4 o'clock.
c You must book—tickets for members are free and tickets for non-members are $10.
d We are opposite the railway station.

2 **a** Ideal holiday entertainment for under 10s.
b Concessions for schoolchildren.
c Book now or miss out.
d All ages welcome but especially suitable for teenagers.

3 c

Word study

1 instrumental
2 communal
3 wearable
4 decorative
5 artistic
6 regional
7 personal
8 creative
9 imaginative
10 skilful (sometimes also spelt 'skillful')

Evaluating other people's writing

Improvements that could be made include the following:

- Space out information—it is too crowded and confusing,—e.g. add line space between main sections of advertisement—after first three lines, after $130.
- Add bullets to make a list of important information.
- Omit unimportant words, e.g. *that's ... in all, I am a ..., for the past ...*
- Highlight phone number at end.
- Perhaps convert some information to questions, e.g. Would you like to learn printmaking?

Quick think

1 editor
2 director
3 driver
4 producer
5 designer
6 actor
7 governor
8 historian
9 juggler
10 mathematician
11 sculptor
12 pianist

Writing paragraphs and whole texts

1 Possible way to write and organise advertisement:

NEPEAN HIGH SCHOOL ART AND CRAFT SHOW

15, 16 and 17 October

Official opening by **Kylie Watson**
(Shauna Bradley in 'Home and Away')
7.30 pm Friday

Open 9 am to 6 pm Saturday, and 9 am to 4 pm Sunday

Feature artist—Blue Mountains artist Fay Graham

NEPEAN HIGH SCHOOL
GREAT WESTERN HIGHWAY, EMU PLAINS

2 Possible way to write and organise advertisement:

EMBROIDERY DISPLAY

Colourful and exciting works by young artists from 5 to 18 years old

Young Textile and Fibre Group of the Embroiderers' Guild, NSW Inc
Saturday 2 October to Sunday 24 October

Official opening by Councillor Angelique Henson
10 am, Saturday 9 October

Works reflect the group's aim to encourage the use of textiles in mixed media and fibre techniques, creative skills and free and imaginative expression using individual ideas and designs.

Braemar Gallery, 104 Macquarie Road, Springwood
Open Friday to Sunday from 10 am to 4 pm,
or by arrangement outside hours

CHAPTER 13: EXPLANATION

Comprehension

1 b

2 because we depend on sight more than any other sense to supply us with information about the world we live in

3

Camera	Eye
viewfinder	cornea
aperture	pupil
lens	lens
film	retina

4 The eyes allow us to make sense of what we see because they are connected to the brain.

5 The brain puts together the information it receives from each eye, it learns to read upside-down images and turn them the right way up, and it sorts out information it receives from the two types of light-sensitive nerve cells.

Writing skills

1 **a** record images onto film
b electrical impulses
c the upside-down images on the retina

- **d** put together the information it receives from each eye, and learn to read upside down images and turn them the right way up

2 *eye/eyes* used 7 times, *camera* used 5 times, *brain* used 5 times

3 The eye is like a camera in many ways. However, there are some important differences. There are two important things the brain does. Firstly it puts together information from each eye and secondly it learns to read upside-down. The brain also sorts out information from two types of nerve cells.

4
- **a** personal opinion not appropriate in factual explanation
- **b** eye problems not relevant here where focus is on how eyes work
- **c** not relevant
- **d** personal information, not relevant to factual explanation

5 *called, allowed in, is controlled, brought, is called, projected, is inverted* (para. 2), *are connected, are formed, are converted, are sent, are converted* (para. 3)

Vocabulary

Nouns: organ, aperture, focus (can also be a verb, but used as noun in the text), membrane, similarity, impulses
Verbs: supply (can also be a noun, but used as verb in the text), projected, inverted, converted, register, disappear
Adjectives: crucial, transparent, optic, meaningful, double, sensitive
Adverbs: particularly, automatically

Focus on punctuation

1. Each main part (or organ) of your body is made of different kinds of cells.
2. The top part of our skin (called the epidermis) wears away as we wash and dry ourselves and move about.
3. Waxy and oily substances are made by tiny glands (called the sebaceous glands) near the hair.
4. A single nerve cell (or neuron) is much thinner than an ordinary electrical wire.
5. One set of nerves carries signals to your brain (the sensory nerves) and one set of nerves carries signals from your brain to your muscles (the motor nerves).

Select a word

1. aperture
2. crucial
3. membrane
4. register
5. transparent
6. converted
7. impulses
8. meaningful

Grammar

1
- **a** P, X-rays **b** A, The Hubble Space Telescope
- **c** A, Blood **d** P, The moon
- **e** P, The first jet-powered flight
- **f** P, Photography **g** A, The skin

2
- **a** The millions of signals are controlled and coordinated by the brain.
- **b** About half your weight is made up by muscles.
- **c** Oxygen is carried to every part of the body by the blood.
- **d** Oxygen is needed by every part of your body.

Word study

1. disconnect
2. misbehave
3. disadvantage
4. misunderstand
5. mislead
6. disobey
7. disapprove
8. disinfect
9. miscalculate
10. disagree
11. misguide
12. misplace

Evaluating other people's writing

Improvements that could be made include the following:

- Add introduction that clearly identifies the thing or process you are explaining.
- Omit personal comment, e.g. *It is brilliant the way the ear works really, but one ear is better than none.*
- Organise information into paragraphs that focus on different aspects of what is being explained.
- Develop some parts with more detail—this explanation contains some very short (even one-sentence) paragraphs.
- Fix sentences that run together: change last paragraph to *The sound goes from the outer ear, which is like an ear trumpet, through the canal and onto the ear drum. It then goes past three tiny bones and through some fluid in the inner ear. Then it is converted to electrical signals.*
- Omit conversational language, e.g. *actually, really*

Quick think

1 a	**2** b	**3** c
4 a	**5** a	

Proofreading

It can store millions of bits of information at the same time (2nd sentence); For example, it records information gathered by our sense of sight and our sense of smell (5th sentence); This is also why we can recognise a smell after a long time (7th sentence); In fact, we have approximately 10 000 million nerve cells (10th sentence).

Writing paragraphs and whole texts

1. g, d, c, b, a, e, f
2. A sample paragraph: Sounds go through many different forms before they reach your brain. They begin as sound waves in the air, but then change to vibrating solids—your eardrum and three tiny bones. Then they become vibrating fluids inside your inner ear. Finally they are converted into electrical impulses and sent along the nerves to your brain.

CHAPTER 14: FACTUAL REPORT

Comprehension

1 b. Reports may include some discussion of the information and ideas it covers, but this should be done in an objective way. The focus is on factual information and, where appropriate, ideas and opinions based on sound evidence.

2 Habitat—para. 3, Conservation efforts—para. 5, Endangerment—para. 4, Characteristics—para. 2
You probably said 'yes'. Paragraphing is commonly used for all but the shortest reports.

3
- **a** para. 3, after first sentence
- **b** para. 2, after first sentence
- **c** para. 4, after last sentence
- **d** para. 2, after fourth sentence

4
- **a** two horns
- **b** an area that the rhino lives in and considers its own
- **c** for their horns, which are used in eastern medicines or as decorative handles
- **d** about 6000
- **e** armed rangers defending game parks, dehorning rhinos to make them valueless, protected sanctuaries, international captive breeding programs

Writing skills

1 a, b, c, d, e

2 after para. 2 or para. 3—after para. 3 would be best; possible headings for paragraph: Diet or Eating habits

3
- **a** its sense of smell
- **b** home ranges
- **c** The International Rhino Foundation
- **d** the rhinos

4
- **a** Correct.
- **b** During its life, a female butterfly lays from 100 to several thousand eggs.
- **c** Wasps take very good care of their young and travel a long way to find just the right insect to feed them.
- **d** Crickets have keen ears, which are located on their legs instead of their heads.
- **e** The ostrich is a strange bird with many odd things about it, but it does not hide its head in the sand.
- **f** Because whales, like all other water mammals, are descended from ancestors who lived on the land, they have had to adapt themselves to life in the water.

5
- **a** advice to reader such as this not relevant in factual report
- **b** not relevant because report is on the African black rhino only
- **c** subjective words that show writer's feeling and attitude (e.g. *cruel*, *butcher*) not appropriate in factual report
- **d** as for c—not appropriate for writer to show own feelings, attitudes or opinions in factual report

Vocabulary

1

dom/in/ant 3	verge 1
ex/tinc/tion 3	pre/dat/ors 3
bound/a/ries 3	en/dang/er/ment 4
cris/is 2	cat/as/troph/ic 4
pro/port/ions 4	ven/er/ab/le 4
dras/tic 2	spec/tac/u/lar 4
poach/ing 2	cer/e/mon/i/al 5
dag/gers 2	in/tense 2
stab/il/is/a/tion 5	sanc/tu/ar/ies 4
en/cour/a/ging 4	mag/nif/i/cent 4

2 Nouns: verge, extinction, predators, boundaries, endangerment, crisis, proportions, daggers, stabilisation, sanctuaries,
Verbs: poaching, encouraging (could also be seen as adjective in the context of the text)
Adjectives: dominant, catastrophic, venerable, drastic, spectacular, ceremonial, intense, magnificent
Adverbs: none

Select a word

1 verge
2 predators
3 dominant
4 proportions
5 venerable
6 drastic
7 sanctuaries
8 encouraging

Grammar

1 The numbers have now stabilised at about 2000. Nevertheless, the poaching threat remains great.
2 Fewer than 200 Sumatran rhinos survive in the wild. Furthermore, there is no indication the situation is stabilising.
3 The black rhino is in fact grey and often assumes the colour of the soil in which it wallows.
4 Over 200 poachers have been killed since 1984. However, poachers have killed 1170 rhinos.
5 The black rhino has a pointed lip. In contrast, the white rhino has a square lip.
6 Endangered species must be protected. Otherwise, we will lose these precious animals forever.

Word study

spectacular: amazing, magnificent, impressive, remarkable, stunning, awe-inspiring
dominant: main, major, primary, principal, chief, predominant, leading
species: breed, class, kind, type, variety
area: environment, region, locality, sector, territory, zone
boundary: border, limit, edge, brink, verge, perimeter

Evaluating other people's writing

Improvements that could be made include the following:

- Add introduction which clearly defines and/or classifies the topic—here the topic seems to be tigers, but the report has two paragraphs that are about the Bengal tiger.

- Organise information so that each section or paragraph is about one aspect only—here information is muddled throughout.
- Add information about other aspects, e.g. appearance, diet.
- Move website address to references at end of text and put name of website in text instead.
- Omit reference to '*we*'—too personal for factual report—perhaps use *human beings, the world,* or *man* instead
- Omit emotional comment about *at least something is being done.*

Quick think

1 a
2 b
3 b
4 b

Writing paragraphs and whole texts

1 a, c, e, d, f, h, g, b

CHAPTER 15: POEM

Comprehension

1 she is a schoolgirl, she goes to an all-girls school (no boys are mentioned), she likes privacy, she feels pressured by school work, she has very negative feelings about other girls at school
2 b
3 **a** dandruff
b rubbish
c imprison
d rejection from a group, being made an outsider
4 **a** to emphasise that she is different from the other girls—not one of them
b the dark of the locker
c teachers and others in authority at school
d bad feeling between the girls (perhaps not talking to each other) because of competition, e.g. getting better marks than someone else
5 The writer appears to feel unhappy about many aspects of life at school and to feel the need to have a private space where she can hide away.

Writing skills

2 *Soggy chips sag in spilt Coke trails*; *caressed/cockroach*; *private places*; *hidden holes*; *savagely shove*; *gossiping gangs and hostile glares*
3 *Caress* is a word we usually use for a loving and sensual embrace from another person. Here it is used to describe how a cockroach (an insect that most people find repulsive) touches the personal belongings of the young girls. Most readers would feel repulsion at the cockroaches being in the locker in the first place, but the use of the word *caress* increases this repulsion, as we imagine the cockroaches lovingly touching the girls' personal belongings.
4 The writer uses different verbs to describe the action of closing the door in each verse—each shows a different feeling; verse 1, *shut* is what most of the girls do— quickly and unthinkingly put their belongings in the locker; verse 2, *close* shows that the writer is more thoughtful than they are about the action (*close* is a gentler action than *shut*)—the locker has her treasures in there and she does not want them disturbed; verse 3, *slam* shows that the writer is angry and upset about school pressures—her action is a bad-tempered reaction to these; verse 4, *lock* shows that her feelings about the other girls are beyond anger—they are more upsetting and slamming the door would not be enough—she needs to keep these burdens away for ever and so locking is the action she needs; the writer also changes the second verb in this verse—*lose the key* instead of *turn the key*—and this verb reinforces the depth of her emotion
5 girls' lockers—She conveys an image of a rubbish dump, e.g. *crusts, crumbs and crumpled cardboard*; *soggy chips sag in spilt Coke trails*; *lollies melt on scurf-clogged haircombs*; *caressed by waving cockroach feelers.*
girls—She conveys an image of cruel behaviour: *spiteful rumours*; *gossiping gangs*; *hostile glares*; *jealous feuds.*

Focus on punctuation

1 The heavy use of punctuation in 'Boy' highlights the separateness and cautiousness of the boy who wants to join in with the others—the full stops and commas break up the text forcing us to read the poem in a slow, halting way, reflecting the boy's slow cautious movements and his puzzlement at why he cannot play.
2 The lack of punctuation in 'Hummingbird' reinforces the quick light movements of the bird itself—it forces us to read the poem quickly, going from one line to the next without pause—just as the hummingbird might flit from one flower to the next.

Select a word

1 caressed
2 debris
3 feuds
4 ostracism
5 hurl
6 hoards
7 savagely
8 myriad

Grammar

1 examples only:
a as dark as a well
b as soft as a kitten's fur
c as strong as an army
d as light as a newborn babe
e as cool as an afternoon breeze

2 examples only:
  a I am deeply depressed.
  b Sleep wraps me up safely as if I was an insect in a cocoon.
  c I am a dancer and I express myself through the movements of my feet.
  d The wind is lashing wildly into me and cutting into my skin.
  e My heart is broken and will never mend.

Word study

1 I am completely sure about something but will take it back if proven wrong.
2 I said something that I should not have (e.g. told something that was a secret) and got myself into an embarrassing situation.
3 She annoys me intensely.
4 He always sees the worst in any situation and never wants to take part.
5 He needs to be extremely careful about what he says or does or he will be in big trouble.
6 Don't make a fuss— just go along with what is happening.
7 Don't do anything stupid.
8 I would do anything for her because I care so much for her.
9 She thinks she is very special—better than anyone else.
10 It was a complete mess.

Evaluating other people's writing

Differences include the following:

- Subject is nature, not personal feelings.
- There is only one verse.
- Structure reinforces the movement of the snake—short, sharp movements, then slow ones.
- There is greater use of alliteration to create the image of the snake.
- There is more focus on actions and appearances.

Similarities include the following:

- Use of language to create images is very effective.
- While it appears on the surface to be a simple, concrete subject, the writer introduces depth and complexity describing her reaction and feeling (last lines).
- Use of rhythm is good.

Quick think

1 Coleridge
2 Donne
3 Tennyson
4 Longfellow
5 Shelley
6 Blake
7 Carroll
8 Lear
9 Hopkins
10 Frost
11 Keats
12 Paterson

Writing paragraphs and whole texts

2 *The night is like an approaching army; an army of stars; it swallows you up; the night weaves its pattern of stars with a giant needle; a needle threading time; it weaves the path to your destiny; the night … waters your thoughts; … bloom like flowers of the night*

Acknowledgements

The author and publisher would like to thank the following for their generous permission to use materials in the book:

- Josh Langerak for the recount 'Adventure World—Design and Technology excursion', Chapter 3
- Kieran Colreavy for the recount 'Down at the Graveyard—Year 9 History excursion', Chapter 3
- Catherine Bendall and Hannah McLean for the recounts, Chapter 3
- Rosie Brown for *Macbeth* imaginative recount, Chapter 3
- Sally Dennis for the book reports on *Tomorrow, When the War Began*, *Z for Zachariah* and *The Silver Crown*, Chapter 5
- William McLean for the description of a scene 'The game', Chapter 6
- Kim Ung for the short story 'The Journey', Chapter 7
- Nick Henderson for the short story, 'Calling home', Chapter 7
- Amber Hopkins for the short story, 'It's all about luck', Chapter 7
- Australian Associated Press, for the newspaper article 'Try to buy before you steal', Chapter 8
- Ellen Connelly for the newspaper article 'Botanic Gardens ritual: it's a blooming mystery', Chapter 8
- Christine Yap for the letter to the editor, 'Hungry for more', Chapter 9
- The *Sun-Herald*, for Christine Yap's letter to the editor, and the newspaper articles, '3000 shine for hungry' and 'Lachlan's surprise visit to see his bride and joy', Chapter 9
- Alli Barnard for the speech on capital punishment, Chapter 11
- Springwood Youth Project for advertisements for Young Women's Music Groups and Wearable Body Art Workshops, Chapter 12
- Out of the Blue Performing Arts Incorporated for advertisement for *Jesus Christ Superstar* auditions, Chapter 12
- Nepean High School for newspaper article 'Art and Craft show', Chapter 12
- Braemar Gallery, Springwood for newspaper article 'Young textile and fibre artists at Braemar', Chapter 12
- *Blue Mountains Gazette* for all advertisements and newspaper articles used in Chapter 12
- Hannah McLean for factual report, 'The Black Rhino', Chapter 14
- Erica Fryberg for poems 'Lockers' and 'The Snake' from *Turns of Phrase*, edited by Lawrie Ryan and Ross Clark, published by University of Queensland Press, 1988, Chapter 15
- Nicole Gardiner for poem 'Hummingbird' from *Turns of Phrase*, edited by Lawrie Ryan and Ross Clark, published by University of Queensland Press, 1988, Chapter 15
- Danielle van Coevorden, Jessie Garbellini, Hannah McLean, Crystalline Cayabyab, and Sophie Holmes for poems in Chapter 15
- Penrith High School, especially Mrs Bernhart, for material from the Penrith High Yearbook and Literary Journal.

Notes

Notes